British Red Cross
Humberside Branch

Mr Eric Williams

DJW/ML/A27

8th March 1994

Dear Mr Williams,

'ON PARADE FOR HIMMLER'

Congratulations on producing such an entertaining
and informative account of your wartime exploits and
your kind recollections of the Society's service.
On behalf of the Humberside Branch of the British Red
Cross I am most grateful for your generous support
in donating part of the proceeds to assist our work
to continue. We wish you every success with the book.

Yours sincerely,

David Whincup
Director

I

ON PARADE FOR HIMMLER

Eric Williams G.C.M.

•

ONE MAN'S STORY OF

SURVIVAL WITH THE

AID OF THE

RED CROSS

RiversEdge

A RiversEdge Publication

RiversEdge Books
Published by RiversEdge
42-43 High Street
Hull HU1 1PS

Printed by The Print Industry
42-43 High Street
Hull HU1 1PS

Body text set in 12 point Century Schoolbook by
The Print Industry
42-43 High Street
Hull HU1 1PS

ON PARADE FOR HIMMLER
by Eric Williams G.C.M.

ISBN 0 9521561 2 1

Cover Design – The Print Industry
Back Cover Photograph – © Eric Williams G.C.M.

Published in the United Kingdom by RiversEdge.

Publishers Note

The publishers wish to point out that the photographs herein, portraying life during Eric's captivity, were taken by professional photographers employed by the German Propaganda Machine.

These pictures were subsequently sold to the prisoners, for cigarettes, they were then encouraged to send them home to reassure their loved ones as proof of their well being. For the most part this was far from the truth, yet served the German Propaganda Machine's purpose.

The publishers felt that these facts should be stressed in order to diffuse the clever illusion that may continue to influence and soften the image of war that future generations may adopt.

Dedication

CALL it the chivalry of total war . . . the influence of Christian standards . . . perhaps just the lowest common denominator of decency among world powers. Whatever the motive that prompted us in 1929 to join with our potential enemies and sign the Geneva Convention – thank God for that document and for the International Red Cross in all its wide ramifications. Without the Red Cross we should have spent our years of captivity lacking comforts, contact with home, a variety of diversions and distractions – even the bare quantity of food necessary to preserve healthy bodies. Instead, we have prospered under its care. In innumerable ways it has been a fairy godmother to us, gradually transforming a strange, wire-bound world, that looked so joyless at the outset, into a place worth living in. That it could never have been a perfect organisation was due to the very circumstances of its existence. But we know that it achieved what it set out to do. Under difficult conditions it brought splendid results. If we have been able to make the slightest constructive use of this interlude between war and peace, if we have merely come through sound in physical and mental condition, then our debt to the Red Cross is one which we can hope neither to repay nor forget. All that we have or hope to be in the years ahead is a part of that debt. What the Red Cross has done for us, and will continue to do for others, is a symbol of an ideal no passing wars will destroy. It will always be our privilege to associate ourselves with that work in every possible way.
May we never fail the Red Cross.

ERIC WILLIAMS, G.C.M.

INDEX

Private Williams.

CHAPTER ONE

Private Williams

WE ARE:
BRITISH..ENGLISH..ANGELSKI..ENGLANDERS..
ANGLICHANI..NOT GERMANS

THIS was to be our regular explanation as we escaped from the German Prison Camps through Russia back to England, but let's start at the beginning... It was in 1937 that my Uncle Walter decided to join the Territorial Army in the Artillery Regiment. He looked splendid in his khaki uniform with brass buttons, flat cap and badges. I was very envious of him. I was only seventeen at the time but the sight of Uncle Walter in his uniform urged me to try and join up. I found to my dismay that I was too young for the Artillery, but I could join the Infantry as a Junior with only partial uniform, until I was eighteen. This I decided to do and reported to Londesborough Barracks. I think that the fact that I was well known as a pianist helped me to pass the initial entry exam, such as they were, and eventually I was issued with my khaki uniform of trousers, jacket (with brass buttons) and a Glen Garrie Cap. I had to use my own shoes and greatcoat as being a junior recruit these items were only issued to the full ranking personnel, it seemed the norm that young recruits would get fed up and leave before signing up for the real thing. Not so for Private Williams. I entered into the life with absolute enthusiasm and never missed a single drill night.

Needless to say, my musical talents as a dance band pianist were well and truly exploited, with the Officers Dances, N.C.O. dances and of course the other Ranks too. I do not think that there were ever as many social occasions as there were, once I had established myself. We had a really good dance band with many of the Hull lads playing along with me.

The Annual Camp at Rolston, near Hornsea was the great event of the year. We would muster at the Barracks, in our uniforms, buttons shining, and be taken in big Army trucks to Rolston where we were allocated our sleeping quarters, in huts housing a dozen men per hut. Food was by the way of the cookhouse and at times, left a little to be desired, but we were happy, learning how to use a rifle, how to throw grenades etc. in case of any war.

My 18th birthday came whilst I was at the camp at Rolston and it was a very proud moment when I was called to 'sign up' for a period of five years with the Territorial Army. At least, I was now on the same level as my Uncle Walter.

I received my year's 'Bounty Money' which was one shilling for every drill night (5p) plus £2.00 for the fortnight's camp. I was rich!!

In 1939, many rumours were flying around and us terriers (as we were called) were itching to 'have a go'. On August 15th a hand delivered letter arrived at my home telling me to report, with full kit, to the Londesborough Barracks at once. My mother wasn't too thrilled at the idea, as she had weird ideas on my activities as a soldier. I think at this stage that I should mention that relations between my mother and I were at times sometimes strained as, being an adopted child from birth, I was in fact a dad's lad, and after my dad's death in 1936, I tended to be somewhat 'in the way' so to speak.

I arrived at the barracks and was issued with a rifle and

bayonet and boarded a very large army lorry, which took us to Easington, where we were put into concrete barracks left over from the 1914-18 war. We were given lectures that if war came, we must be prepared to guard Spurn Peninsular, against any invaders.

We were given bayonet practice with strung up sand bags (I was not too good at this I would add).

On September 3rd 11.00am, it was announced over the radio that Germany had invaded Poland and that we were now at war with Germany.

I felt a moment of panic come over me. It was alright us talking big and saying lets have a go at them...we will show them etc. but NOW, IT WAS HERE, the Germans were most probably saying the same...what if they were stronger than us?...

I think that our fears were spotted by our Senior Officers, most of them regular soldiers, who got us all together for a morale boosting session, which I must admit did help...after all if the German tanks were only made out of cardboard our bullets would easily penetrate them, plus the fact that we had had years of training, where as the Germans comprised of Hitler Youth Boys and this leader of theirs called Adolf Hitler was only a house painter after all...he was not even a soldier. And we believed it all!

I was sent down to the tip of Spurn Point where we had ten days on and ten days off. We had two spells at Bull Fort, which was a Fort in the middle of the Humber used during World War One. Not a very pleasant experience, as the Fort was cold and very damp.

I did not mind the guard duties at Spurn Point, but one day I asked our Sergeant whose name was Sergeant Fulcher, 'Sergeant, what do we do if the Germans do come?' His reply was 'Don't ask daft questions laddie...'I never did really find out...We were a happy lot at Spurn, but I must admit we seemed to concentrate on our entertainments a lot more than the impending war issues. We had most of the well known local entertainers, including the very well known comedian Jimmy Welsh, Alec Rebera on drums, and many other singers, mouth-organ players, and a good assortment of various musicians. We managed to form a band of sorts and provided good entertainment for the lads. The Crown and Anchor at Kilnsea was well patronised and was reached by a very small railway that travelled up and down the Spurn Peninsular, its main intention to carry supplies down to the Point for us troops. The remnants of this tiny railway track are still there to this day.

In November, we were sent to Stow on the Wold...we occupied a gorgeous Manor, which was sacrilege in itself. We soon had a good dance band going and performed quite often at the Town Hall...free dances for the civvies...great, I like the War!

In January 1940 we were told that we would be leaving Stow and going over the sea to France as the B.E.F. (British Expeditionary Force), as it was likely that the Germans were going to invade France. Again that little niggle of panic rose inside me. Our Officers soon dispelled any fears that we had...they were great. We had Colonel Robson with us, of Moors and Robson Breweries, who could not be classed as the greatest of leaders, except to the canteen and the bar, where he was always to be found.

CHAPTER TWO

Wooden bullets and cardboard tanks

WE landed at Cherbourg and were taken to a small village called Thoix a few miles outside of Lille. We occupied a farm house's out buildings, the local school and many other buildings in the village, the local Estaminet was very well patronised and both the local girls and us got on very well indeed.

Again, we had our morale boosters...don't worry lads, you have nothing to fear etc!!

We were all issued with one clip of bullets for our rifles, this comprised of a dozen bullets made up of two tracer bullets, three live bullets and seven wooden nosed bullets which only made a noise and would not have killed a fly. This was what we went to war with...but we were told, don't worry, the Germans have got less than us.

It was the middle of May...glorious weather and our spell in France was most certainly very enjoyable. We were ordered to carry our rifles at all times, even to the cafe, even to the toilet...and it was on one of these glorious mornings that we were being given a pep talk by one of the Officers outside our favourite cafe when one of our despatch riders came tearing down the street to say that tanks were coming. Our officers said that they were sure they would be British tanks as he had not heard of any impending advancement of the enemy. And he carried on with his lecture. Suddenly, we heard the sound of a large motor coming our way. Johnny Minster who was a good pal of mine suddenly shouted, 'there's a tank at the end of the street'. Our Officers said 'I'm sure that it will be one of ours'. We could clearly see the big black cross on the front of the tank by now...Charlie, another mate, said 'It's an effin Jerry!' Johnny Minster who was sat next to me, grabbed his rifle and said 'I'm not effin waiting to find out...' I replied 'me neither' and we ran for cover. We ran over the fields to a dry ditch and took cover, rifles at the ready, officers and all. Then they came, Christ, they were not cardboard tanks and the German Soldiers on top of the tanks and running beside them were armed to the teeth. We very quickly knew that it would be suicide to stay where we were so our Officers told us to make our way across the fields to the beach at Boulogne. This we did...I never knew that I could run so fast. Bullets whizzed by us pinging away. I saw six or seven of our lads had been hit by the oncoming force, but we managed to get to Boulogne and scrambled down the cliffs into a disused railway tunnel. At least we were out of the Germans fire. A group of French soldiers soon joined us and we decided that we would make a stand for it and that three British lads would be at the entrance for two hours, guarding the tunnel, followed by two hours from the Froggies. Brave me, I volunteered for the first shift along with Johnny and another mate. Nothing happened.

The Frogs took over after our stint and after half an hour had passed, a very young German Soldier poked his head around the tunnel and without further to do, every single French man raised his hands into the air in an act of surrender. So one very young Jerry made his capture of at least thirty British and fifty French soldiers. He shouted for his German comrades to come down and they were amazed to see us all neatly rounded up without a shot being fired!

I had my S.B. arm band on (meaning that I was a stretcher bearer and Medical man) so I was given the task of looking after the wounded. The rest were marched off and I was left with about eight wounded lads from my own regiment. Luckily we all had our Army Field Dressings, so I was able to patch up as best as I could. Two of the lads had abdominal wounds, which apart from putting a pad over the wound I could do nothing. One lad died in my arms.

Two hours passed and a group of Germans came into the tunnel, to say that they would be looking after the wounded and promised to get them to hospital. (After the War I found out that they did carry out this promise and that the lads were treated very well in the Boulogne Hospital which the Germans commandeered). I was marched along with a lad that had only a slight nick, to join the rest of the gang who had been captured and we were 'marched' through Boulogne, the French civillians jeered at us and we saw many of the local French girls arm in arm with the German soldiers. The French would not give us water, although the Jerries made some of them give us water. As we marched through the streets of Boulogne, there were hundreds of dead British soldiers...the remains of one hell of a battle. It was the most demoralising sight that I have ever witnessed. Young British lads lying everywhere, some with half a head missing, another with his guts strewn over the road, it was a sight of a nightmare. All German dead had been removed, just the British and a few, and I mean a few, French left for the flies to feast on.

We were ushered up the hill to the outskirts of Boulogne and into a field where we were told we would stay the night. We had no food, no water. We were a very dejected remnant of the British Expeditionary Force, sent out to halt any German advance into France. We never stood a chance.

CHAPTER THREE

Stalag 17

WE marched through France and we managed to survive by grabbing turnips or potatoes from the fields...village pumps were our source of water ...we had no food from the Germans...they had none for themselves...and the French were very hostile toward the British, giving us nothing. Occasionally, we managed to get a little bread, which was shared out, from some friendly French. The story was the same as we entered Belgium, although the Belgium people were very friendly towards us, just the opposite to the French. Finally we were put onto trucks to take us to a marshalling point for British Prisoners of War at a town called Trier.

Trier, as far as I can recollect, was a lovely town, although at the time I was in no state to appreciate it, plus the fact that red flags bearing the Swastika were hanging from every building. The Trier people did not like the British and did everything possible to show it...refusing us water, hurling stones and obvious German abuse at us. We were glad to be put in cattle trucks to be taken to the Prisoner of War camps set up for us somewhere in Poland. We were three days in these cattle trucks with no food and very little water. There was nowhere for us to go to the toilet and by the end of the three days we absolutely stank. Four British lads had died in the truck that I was in, through sheer starvation and depravation. It was a miracle that any of us survived by the time we arrived at our destination.

Finally the train stopped and the doors were unlocked and we were told in no uncertain terms to get out...Schnell

schnell British Swinen. We were lined up and counted and finally a German Commandant who spoke perfect English got up and made a speech to us saying...'You are now prisoners, and for you, the war is over. If you behave yourselves and work well you will be treated well until we have won the war then we will send you back to your families in England which will be run by the German Government'.

We were marched to a prison camp which was very heavily guarded with miles of barbed wire round it, and patrols of Jerries with very vicious looking dogs going round the perimeter of the camp. There were wooden huts with three tier bunks and straw mattresses, and they were very crowded.

As I entered the hut, the air was thick and polluted with smoke from the stench of burning wood on numerous small fires burning on the bare earth which was the floor of the hut. The smell of sweaty flesh from unwashed bodies, and the stagnant air was nauseating to say the least. There were these small fires in tins, home made contraptions, with men crouching over them, cooking frugal meals in an endeavour to satisfy the aching pains of hunger. The cooking utensils were old herring tins with improvised handles. No fires were allowed outside of the hut for fear of attracting enemy aircraft.

We were the new arrivals, ignorant of the ways of Stalag 17. We were soon to learn, and in some cases, learn the hard way. I asked where the toilets were. This brought a few laughs, but I was pointed to the so-called toilets which comprised of a single pole strung over a ditch, with another pole a little higher up to rest one's back on. We had to sit in a row defacating and urinating en mass...no toilet paper, no privacy and absolutely no effort to maintain any degree of hygiene.

It was to get worse. Warmer weather brought hordes of flies to breed in that devil's ditch. The stench grew worse, the flies did their work and very soon dysentry was rampant.

We were allowed in an ice cold shower once a week. We were told to parade outside a large building and strip off, we were crawling with lice and we had not had a change of clothes or a bath for months. We were told to go into this building and have a shower and our clothes would be put into an oven to kill all the lice. As we went into the building we were given a piece of brownish looking soap measuring 1" by 2" and 1/4" thick to share between six men. We stood under the jet heads waiting for the water to come through for over half an hour. A daft jerry poked his head in to see if we had finished. The silly goon had forgotten to turn the water on. The water did eventually come through and it was absolutely freezing cold, but we did have the shower. We were then ushered out of the building (still starkers) and we had to dry off in the sun. We could smell our uniforms baking...yuk! About two hours later (still in the nifty) the jerries arrived on a lorry with clothes, they turned out to be Polish uniforms and we had no option but to put them on. Our officers protested but the Germans were not interested. At least we had got rid of the lice.

Life in this camp was dreadful, and to say that we just existed, sums it up in one. We had no shoes so the Germans gave us wooden clogs with bits of cloth to wrap around our feet to try and stop blistering. We were a dejected lot at an all time low...there seemed to be no news of the end of the war, and it seemed at times that the world had forgotten us. Many of our lads died through sheer starvation, depravation and the varied ailments that were rampant in the camp. It was survival of the fittest, and those of us that maintained the very will to live, survived. Our main thoughts were that we would beat the bastards, and every day was a battle of wits against the enemy to out-do them in any way...Life was VERY hard.

We stayed in this camp for 2 years, living on the barest of rations. The food dished out to us was half a litre of cabbage, turnip, or potato soup, plus 3 slices of black bread per day. The soup was cooked in huge cauldrons and one always tried to get to the middle of the queue so that the resulting soup I received would be from the bottom of the cauldron, thereby being just that little bit thicker.

Bored with talking and listening to unfounded rumours, I would climb into my bunk to close my eyes and lapse into the world of fantasy and escape this Hell of reality. Day after day, it was the monotony of hunger, lice and an everlasting bid for survival. I will carry the scars of those lice to my dying day.

I noticed that my flesh was leaving my bones, my thighs had lost their solid packing and my legs were spindly, the area from my ankles up was virtually devoid of skin, just a mass of running sores, thanks to the ever present lice.

We did, however, devise a plot to put the damned lice to work for us. We collected them in little boxes and every time a guard came past a bunk the one on the top bunk would empty the box on to the hat of the guard, thereby ensuring that the great German Army got a good share of the lice.

CHAPTER FOUR

Our first parcels

ALL of a sudden, one day, the Germans lined us up, and the English speaking Commandant said that a delegation from the Swiss Red Cross would be visiting the camp the following week and he hoped that we had no complaints. He regretted that we would not be allowed to talk with the delegation, but one of the British Officers could meet them. That night instead of the watery soup for supper, we had German sausage, margarine for the bread and erzatz caffee (coffee made out of roasted barley). The next day, we had music played over the loud speakers by a fantastic German dance band called Peter Kreuder. We were issued with extra soup and again sausage for the main meal...obviously they were 'buttering' us up for the Red Cross visit. Then we were given British uniforms and boots. That was a shot in the arm for us as we hated looking so damned scruffy in the old Polish uniforms. Some of the uniforms were far too big or small but with a bit of swapping and changing we managed to look something like the remnants of the British Army.

The great day arrived and we were lined up but instead of us being English Schwinehund, we suddenly were called 'Tommy' or 'Englisher Soldat'. The delegation arrived, and under very close supervision by the Jerries, inspected us, the huts, and asked the Officer what the conditions were like. He told them 'bloody awful', lack of proper food, sanitation and next to nil medical facilities. He complained that we were overcrowded and insisted that the delegation saw the graves of the British Soldiers who had died through sheer starvation. The Germans were furious, but the Swiss leader of the delegation reminded the German Officer that the British had many German prisoners in England, and if they reported these facts to the British Government, retaliation would surely be taken. The Swiss Officer asked if we had received the Red Cross parcels and they were told that we had not had anything. It eventually came out that these parcels had been sent from England, but the Germans had stolen them.

After the delegation had left it was once again back to the watery soup and we were once again 'Englisher Schwinehunds'...until about three weeks later when three lorries turned up at the camp gates loaded with Red Cross parcels, plus bulk food to be used for meals. Each of us received a Red Cross Parcel, full of the things we had dreamed about...chocolate, butter, marmite cubes, corned beef, tea, cocoa, coffee and a tin containing soap. From that moment, the Germans attitude to us changed...'they had always done their best for the English Tommies'...and instead of us being called Schwinehunds, we found that they accepted being called 'Square headed bastards'. Usually, in the evening we were locked up in our huts, but now the doors were left open and Jerries would come in to barter for chocolada (chocolate) for eggs or white bread. After a few months of Red Cross food inside of me, I soon began to put on weight and my emaciated legs and arms filled out with re-vitalised flesh. There was now a reason to live – not just exist.

It was then decided by the Vermacht, that they must do something about the overcrowding before the delegation came back, so we were lined up and asked what trades we had, we were a motly lot, we had joiners, bricklayers, a bag-pipe maker (who still had his bag pipes) and I classed myself as a musician (Klavier spieler). We had heard that all trades etc. would be sent to a much better camp, so I kept my fingers crossed that I would be classed as a trade.

Success, a Klavier Spieler (Piano player) was a trade so I joined the party ready to move to the new camp...God knows where it would be.

The great day arrived, we were all packed up with our Red Cross food and we were ushered into cattle trucks...not so bad as the previous experience, as these had seats and a loo, which one sat on and the results just went onto the railway lines below...it was very draughty!

We finally arrived at the new place called Thorun and met our new German Officers and guards. They tried to come the heavy with loos loos schnell etc. by now we could all speak a lot of German and our Officers told them in no uncertain terms that we were British soldiers, as they were German soldiers, that both sides had to do what they were told in the War, we were humans and not pigs and that mis-demeanours on their side would be reported to the Swiss Red Cross. A German guard who had come up with us from the other camp had very quick words with the officers, assuring them that we did have the Red Cross Protection under the Geneva Convention and the attitude of our new guards changed immediately.

We were marched through Thorun singing such ridiculous songs as 'We're Going To Hang Out Our Washing On The Siegfried Line', 'Run Rabbit Run' etc. and the Poles looked on in amazement...How could people like us show such cheerfulness whilst under the mighty Germans? To us they were a load of square heads. We finally arrived at a grim looking Fort surrounded by a dry moat which we crossed over by the draw bridge. There were Jerry guards at both sides so it looked as though escape was just about impossible. In the centre of the Fort was a compound where we were led and a rather vicious looking Jerry with a huge scar down his face (we called him scarface), read out the riot act to us. We had heard it all before. He told us how the glorious Third Reich was winning the War and that soon they would be landing in England and then we would be able to go home to our families in the new England, it seemed that this was a speech for all officers of the German Army that had contact with the British. One lad started singing 'There'll Always Be An England' and gradually we all joined in and to our amazement the Jerry shouted 'yar sing Tommies we want you to be happy here.'

We were allocated our rooms in the Fort and we found that we had six men to a room sharing three double bunk beds, this was marvellous compared with what we had had for the past two and a half years, and with our new uniforms, we had got rid of the lice.

CHAPTER FIVE

Fort 13

LIFE was quite good at Fort 13, made good by the fact
that the Jerries realised that their bartering days
would cease if they did not come to our way of
thinking. Scarface, we learned, was all mouth and was the
biggest racketeer in the German Army. Everytime our Red
Cross Parcels came he would be round in the evening with a
little Corporal carrying a sack of loaves of white bread etc.
and he had a list of things that he wanted. We always had the
upper hand as no-where in Germany could anyone obtain
real coffee or soap like the British soap, and chocolate was
unheard of, so we could name our price for the things he
wanted (obviously to re-sell outside).

In the Fort, I found that there was a lot of good musicians,
some found paper to write music on to pass the time away,
but we had no instruments, so I suggested to the lads we try
to get the piano out of Scarface. The next time he came
round no one wanted his bread or eggs and he was very
upset. He eventually came to our room when he started his
patter and we told him to...OFF. Poor Scarface was nearly in
tears he had obviously got 'orders' for certain items and he
was getting nowhere fast. He asked of me, 'what is wrong? I
am a good German and I help you Tommies, and now no one
wants to do gesheft (business) with me! (one of the lads
remarked that he could not be a good German as he was still
alive). As he was going out of the door, I shouted to him,
come back and lets have some geshefts (lets do some
business). He came back in and I offered him an English
cigarette and a cup of very good coffee (deliberately made
for him). He offered me bread and eggs and when I said I had

enough bread and eggs, he said what gesheft did I want? I said 'We want a Klavier (piano) and until we get one, we will have no more gesheft' He replied 'what in Himmel did we want a piano for?' so we told him we wanted to form a dance band and have concerts with music and he and his German officers could come to them for entertainment. He thought we were mad...Alles Englanders zind Ferikt (all Englishmen are mad).

We told him that he would perhaps get the Iron Cross for his efforts to keep the Englanders happy and thankfully he was daft enough to swallow that one. He went away saying that he would see what he could do, so as a gesture of goodwill we traded his bread and eggs for what he required.

The following week he came and said that he could get a piano, but it would cost a thousand English cigarettes, coffee, chocolate and other valuable items. We told him that we would have a meeting with our British Officers and let him know. We saw our commanding Officer, a Colonel McKie, a true Scot, from one of the Scottish Regiments. He agreed with Scarface, in so much as he too thought we were bloody mad, but he agreed we could do as we wished as long as we didn't fraternise with the enemy. I often wondered where he thought his boiled eggs and white bread came from.

To cut a long story short, we eventually came to a price for the piano and lo and behold a German armoured vehicle trundled across the draw bridge of the Fort with our piano strapped to it and a beaming Scarface sat beside it. We very quickly unloaded it and I ran my fingers over the keys. Christ!! What a noise, where had he dug this antique from I could never imagine any tune coming out of this thing. It had a tattered lace front with protruding candlesticks and half of the damper pedal was missing. It must have been 100 years old. Suddenly, a Welsh voice came out of the crowd of onlookers saying 'let me have a look at it, I am a piano tuner and repairer'. It was like a voice from heaven. Taffy had the monster for a week working on it all day and eventually he invited us to come and have a look at it. I tried it, I could not believe my ears, it was in tune and so the Stalag 13 Dance Band was born. Various instruments were purchased with cigarettes until we had a good 10 piece band. We manufactured a string bass with a wooden box, long piece of string and I believe that a member of the Welsh Guards managed to play it quite well. Instruments that we could not barter for, we managed to get from the Swiss Red Cross who made frequent visits to the camp.

The dance band, with myself at piano.

The Jerries let us convert a dis-used store room into a theatre and it did not take us very long to make a stage with lighting effects, curtains and seating for the hundred or so audience. Every week, I would put on a piano evening and every other week we would put on a Band Show with an array of talent from the camp. Including singers and comedians (and there were plenty of those). And about once a month we would put on a play or a musical show of some description. The Germans realised that it was in their interest to help us with our entertainment as this in turn provided them with entertainment. We had some really good talent among us and this included the very well known actor Sammy Kydd, who after the war became quite a T.V. personality. He produced many good plays which included such well known plays as 'Thark' 'The Dover Road' and 'Journey's End', and our entertainment owed a lot to his talents. The Germans were always keen to take pictures of our various plays, concerts etc., and encouraged us to send them home to England, thus helping the German propaganda.

Programmes for our musical shows.

The theatre was always well supported, especially by the German Officers who in turn helped us to obtain the many things that were needed for the theatre. We were not allowed to play the National Anthem, but we easily substituted that with 'There'll Always Be An England', 'Rule Britannia' or 'Land of Hope and Glory'. The Jerries did not like these tunes or the way that we sang them so they always made an exit during them, but at least we were abiding by the rules of no National Anthem. One tune which we completely tabooed was 'We'll Meet Again' – it caused such emotional upset amongst the lads that we decided to boycott that particular tune. I used to have Request Nights and Colonel McKie our camp C.O. always requested 'A Nightingale Sang In Berkley Square'. I had played it a few times in England, but I'm damned if I could remember the middle eight bars, so I'm afraid that the Colonel got a rather bodged up version of his particular favourite song.

We put on a band concert one evening with the Swiss Delegation present and they were very impressed by our efforts and wanted to know if they could help in any way. I told them that we could do with some new music as we had to keep on playing the same old tunes over and over again. They said that they would try and help. About a month later a censored parcel arrived containing lots of music all written for a sixteen piece band. Although we only had a ten piece band, we decided to have a go with the music. It was all hand written for four saxes and three trumpets (we only had one of each). We spent a long time looking through the music and had several attempts to decipher it, unfortunately, we had to give it up as a bad job. A few of the titles (which we had never heard of) were 'Moonlight Serenade', 'In the Mood' and 'String Of Pearls'. We noticed that they were arranged for an orchestra called 'The Glen Miller Orchestra' never heard of them either. I'm afraid that Mr. Miller's music was never played by us! – so it was back to the music of Harry Roy, Billy Cotton and such tunes as 'Home on the Range' etc.

We had never heard of Glen Miller.

CHAPTER SIX

Padre Wild

L IFE continued to be reasonably good, the Red Cross
parcels came through regularly, some from Canada,
some from Australia, all had varying contents which
were a godsend to us. Without these parcels we would never
have lived through the war and the Germans attitude to us
would have been much different.

We had to work on various things, I worked on a railway
laying new tracks etc., and this way we met quite a lot of
Poles. At this stage I think I ought to mention that all of us
British thought that the Jerries were doing the Poles a lot of
good, as the Polish methods of transport, roads, railways
etc., were about a hundred years behind the times. They still
ploughed the fields with oxen and every Poles ambition in
life was to own a few chickens. The chicken was a Poles
symbol of prosperity and also his means of bartering, with
eggs etc. The blackest black market was definitely in Poland.
We found the Poles to be the biggest racketeers alive,
bartering anything for such things as tea, coffee, soap etc.

We had a Chaplain in our Fort, called Padre David Wild, he
came from Eton College and at the start of the war he had
volunteered to join the Army as a Chaplain and we became
good friends as he too played the piano. We often played
duets together. He would often ask us if we could get
together a few eggs or a loaf of white bread in exchange for
some coffee or something as the Officers had no contact with
the Poles or Scarface come to that, so they had to survive on
the German rations, plus the Red Cross Parcels. They were
very glad of the odd egg or two. The Germans did not class

him as a 'Fighting Officer' and he seemed to get a few more privileges than the other officers did. He was allowed out of the Fort with a guard to go into the town for walks etc.

The Padre was quite a popular person, in so much that he had little time for the Germans (who he christened the Goons) and if any of us were in trouble with the Goons, Padre Wild would always endeavour to sort things out and act as comforter to those of us that had troubles at home. Many married prisoners had word from home that their wives had gone off with someone else...it was a long war.

We did try to keep clean and act like British soldiers. I am seated second from the left.

The Padre was allowed to visit other camps in the surrounding area and was permitted to take one other P.O.W. with him as batman/companion. It was on one of his visits to another camp that he chose me to accompany him and for me it was like going on holiday for a week. The Padre would go to a certain camp and have a talk with the lads, hold a service, have communion and we would usually stay the night. An old guard accompanied us, although what he could have done if we wanted to escape leaves little to the imagination. I played hell with this old guard because he was so damned scruffy, much to the Padres amusement. We always tried to look and behave like British soldiers, even though at times this did prove rather difficult, as I am sure that the great Third Reich populace had never heard of shoe polish.

An incident at one of the camps which we visited, always remains with me. We came to this particular camp to find that another camp was also expecting us. We had only sufficient time left to visit one camp, so I had the bright idea that the Padre should visit the main camp and I should go on to the next one with our little guard and explain the situation to them. This, to the Padre, seemed a good solution, so off we went on our different ways.

I arrived at the camp which had about twenty men working there doing farm work, explained the situation to them, and all was well. The lads had made a feast of a meal, consisting of bacon, eggs, mushrooms and potatoes. It would seem that they lived very well on this farm. The farmer was a German, but looked kindly on his 'free' workers and the lads were certainly having a very comfortable 'war'. There were quite a few romances blossoming with the Polish girls at this particular camp which neither the Jerry farmer, nor the guard took any notice of. Lucky sods!

I duly met up with the Padre the next morning and it would appear that he too had been treat like royalty. So it was the end of my very nice trip and back to the Fort.

One day we were told by the Germans that a Polish Officer by the name of Felix would be staying with us and would be billeting with our Officers. Evidently this Polish Officer had a factory in Poland before the war making Erzats (immitation) rubber, but during the German onslaught in Poland, his factory had been burned down. The Jerries had tried all ways to obtain the formula out of Felix for his rubber, without success, so after years of trying to extract his secrets from him, by varying methods i.e. imprisonment, torture, depravation, they decided to put him with British Officers to try and soften him up.

Each week he was taken away and interrogated by the Germans, without success and eventually he was given a direct ultimatum of seven days to come up with the formula or be taken away from the security of the British, to Gestapo H.Q.

It was during this particular week that David Wild (our Padre) asked us to try and spare a few cigarettes, chocolates etc. for a special reason...we did not ask questions. He made quite a few trips into town with his little German and we wondered what the Hell he was up to, especially with him scrounging things which were most un-Padre like.

On the Saturday morning all Hell broke loose. FELIX WAS GONE, ESCAPED. Within an hour the whole Fort was teaming with Gestapo searching the place from top to bottom for clues. When one of them picked up an empty cigarette packet we would give a loud cheer which annoyed the Gestapo intensely. We were eventually confined to our rooms and as punishment, no Red Cross parcels for a month.

About six weeks later, we were all on morning roll call (the Jerries counted us every morning) and after the roll call, David Wild asked the Jerries if he could say a special prayer as it was a very special day. We wondered what he was up to as it was not a Sunday and he made us sing a hymn (can't remember what it was) then after that he started to give a sermon, with the Jerries looking on very suspiciously, right in the middle of his sermon he simply said that he had some very important news from home, he had had a letter from his wife to say that, the cat who had been away so long had managed to return home. God Bless you all. We knew instantly that he meant Felix (as all cats were called Felix in Poland), so again much to the amazement of the Jerries a loud cheer went up from us all. One German Officer asked 'Vas is loos' (what is happening) and we replied that we were only happy. Again he pronounced that the English were MAD. (Alles Englanders zind ferickt).

It came that Padre Wild had in fact bribed the guards with our precious Red Cross items and had contacted the Polish Underground Movement, who in turn, after a lot of bribing, had managed to smuggle Felix out of the Fort, got him through Poland and eventually into Switzerland and to England. It was pointed out to us that this method of escape could only be used in extreme circumstances, as it involved a lot of planning, bribing and if anything had gone wrong a lot of lives would be lost as the Germans would shoot on sight without hesitation.

We did try several escapes without success...it was hopeless, as we had no maps, or compasses and we did not know where to go, what direction etc.

CHAPTER SEVEN

Six, 3-minute rounds

LIFE went on at Fort 13, our dance band progressed
with us composing melodies to make a change from
Billy Cotton & Co. We had some excellent musicians
in the camp and in case you wonder why so many musicians
were captured, I would point out that all Army musicians
automatically became stretcher bearers during active
service so that they could entertain the troops, and they were
excused guard duty as it was pointless having a band or
concert party if half of the members were on guard duty, so
you see, being a musician had its compensation. Naturally,
being a stretcher bearer of a 'Medical Room' N.C.O. like
myself, meant that one always stayed with the wounded and
risked inevitable capture.

Band shows and variety shows every week. Note my thin arms as I am seated
at the piano.

Often life in the Fort would grow very monotonous and on many occasions tempers would fray and it was on such an occasion that a certain Corporal from the Northumberland Fusiliers Regiment decided to try taking the mickey out of me, referring to my outings with the Padre, also my musical achievements etc, Walker was his name...and it soon ended up with him and me having a scrap.

Our man of confidence (chosen by us to represent us with the Goon etc.) knew of this and tried to put a stop to it, as there seemed to be groups who were now ganging up on each other. He suggested that we had a proper contest in a boxing ring to fight it out. I agreed. Walker also agreed.

This was put to the camp German Feldfeble, who promised to procure two pairs of boxing gloves for the event and he would also provide ropes to make a boxing ring. The date was set for three weeks. It was then found out that four other couples who had grudges etc. also wanted to have a go. So the event was organised.

The ring.

Guardsman Alf Watson (my trainer/manager).

I will be perfectly honest and tell you here and now that the thought of me going into a boxing ring absolutely petrified me. There was no need for any laxatives over the next three weeks, I assure you.

A six foot Guardsman, named Alf Watson decided to become my 'Manager' and Alf and I became firm friends. He had me training every day and showed me how to defend myself, how to use my arms as guards etc. although I do believe that he thought the task was pretty hopeless. I was no fighter!

The day arrived. All the German guards helped to create the boxing ring. They were looking forward to this event. A couple of our lads took bets, but I do not think many bet on me winning. Alf said to me 'look Eric, go in there and give him all you've got'...'even if you get a good pasting, make sure that he gets one too'. This seemed good sense to me and gave me a wee bit of confidence.

Myself.

There were two fights before mine and Walker's, which ended in a draw. A German Unter Officer had been chosen as referee for my fight, (he was a keep fit bloke in the German army) so we climbed into the ring. A good round of applause came for Walker and surprise, surprise a cheer for me. This bucked me up. The ref brought us together and gave us the usual talk. I went back to my corner amid further cheers of 'come on Williams knock hell out of the clever little sod'. I realised that a lot of the crowd were actually bulling for me. Alf in my corner said 'knock shit out of him'. The bell sounded (a tin lid). I was up, now not caring one way or the other. If I was going to get a good hiding I was going to make sure that Walker got one too.

I think the first round was a bit of a fiasco with us both flaying our arms about but doing no damage whatever.

Round Two. After a bit of a talk with Alf, I went out with a lot of confidence. I did exactly what I had been taught to do and used my arms to guard myself and I know that I did get a few punches in, which I think surprised Walker.

Round Three. I had not been hit YET, so I decided to make this a fight. I know this was not the right thing to do, but I had had enough of this larking about and the lads were yelling for more action.

Round Four. I came out of my corner like a miniature rocket and landed a purler. There was blood all over. Christ, I thought, where has he hit me? Then I realised it was not my blood, but Walkers – I had busted his nose! I could hardly believe it, the lads in the crowd were going wild, even the stupid Jerries were shouting VEELUMS VEELUMS. I think that I got a bit over confident as I suddenly felt my bottom lip tasting like jelly...he had landed a good one on me.

Round Five. I was feeling a bit weary now and I noticed that Walker was not so energetic as before. I tried to really get in but I am afraid that four years of P.O.W. life was now taking its toll and I was feeling very fragile.

Round Six. The final Round. Shit or bust now. I gave it all that I had, a warning from the ref about holding, also another warning about hitting low. It seemed an eternity waiting for the final bell to go and when it did, I thankfully walked over to my corner where a delighted Alf was full of praise for putting up such a show. The crowd cheered and a couple of Jerries came over and patted me on the shoulder...The referee declared it was a good fight and that it was a draw. Walker came over to me and said 'I'll get you for busting my nose'. As I knew that I could now stand up to him, I told him, 'anytime you like; NOW IF YOU WANT TO'.

Our man of confidence saw what was happening and straight away put a big STOP to any further arguing. I was quite chuffed, after all I was supposed to be destined for the camp hospital after Walker had finished with me, but instead had come out of it reasonably well. At least I thought so.

The next day I felt very bruised but inwardly, very happy.

CHAPTER EIGHT

Himmler's visit

IT was a couple of months after Felix's escape that it was announced that Herr Himmler was to make a visit to the Fort. Himmler was chief of Gestapo and also had a lot to do with the propaganda of Germany. We asked why he was visiting us and were told that he would be writing a propaganda item in the Deutches Zeitung (The German Newspaper) Colonel McKie had us on parade and told us that we must show this German gentleman (or similar unprintable words) that we were British soldiers and he (the Colonel) would expect to see us on Parade as we would do for a British Officer. We thought that this was a good idea and could be a bit of a laugh, after all we couldn't care less about Himmler, to us he was just another square-head, so the next few days saw us cleaning buttons, those that had them, cleaning their cap badges, trousers were pressed, by way of damping the trouser creases and rubbing soap along the crease line. The trousers were laid under the straw mattress all day and night to press and the result was a knife edge crease that any soldier would be proud of. It did, however mean that we had to go without our trousers for a full day which caused quite a lot of concern among our German guards, who gave the usual remarks that 'Du ferfluckter Englanders sind alles ferickt' (you bloody Englishmen are all completely mad). I must admit that the sight of 300 Englishmen all walking around with no trousers on must have caused quite a lot of concern, and we could see the funny side of our antics. Also boots were cleaned although there was a distinct lack of boot polish. I must confess that when the day arrived for Herr Himmler to arrive we most certainly did look like a vague resemblance of the British army. We lined up on parade. We had all agreed long before this event that seniority would come from the senior regiments...the guards would be I/C and we accepted the orders and discipline from the varied ranks of the guards...from the Colonel to the Regimental Sergeant Major (have you ever met an R.S.M. from the guards?) you see them at the Cenotaph giving the orders. This particular R.S.M. was in our terms 'army barmy'. He lived for the army, his whole life was the army and for him to get us scruffy lot on parade, looking our best, I would add, must have brought joy to the stone which was in place of his heart.

The Colonel looked splendid in his kilt, Jock was there at the ready with his bag-pipes, Padre Wild had his dog collar on and looked very much a vicar and we were all spick and span, every man shaved and looking his best.

The camp Commandant came in and shouted 'Achtung!' to which he got a chorus of jeers all ending with ...OFF. The Colonel and the R.S.M. told us to shut up and play it their way as they could see a lot of trouble if Herr Himmler's toes were trodden on. We simmered down. Then, into the compound strutted this little German twit, with metal spectacles on (I will always remember those horrible spectacles). He acted as though he was going to completely take over but the Colonel was having none of it. He brought us to attention turned and saluted Himmler...by this time Himmler was in a daze and just did not know what to do. Then Jock started to play his bag-pipes...Scotland the Brave ...Himmler looked at the Colonel and in a frenzy asked 'was ist das frauen (woman) Soldaten?' The Commandant explained that the Colonel was a Scotlander and for occasions such as this they wore kilts instead of trousers. The German Commandant was absolutely terrified of Himmler.

The Colonel accompanied Himmler and other German Officers and insisted on an inspection of the troops. This confounded Himmler who had come to hurl insults at us and try and degrade us, instead our Colonel had completely turned round so that we had a distinct advantage over the situation. Very clever.

On parade and smartening up for Himmler.

At the end of the Colonel's tour of inspection of the troops with the German entourage, Himmler tore the Germans into little strips for not being as smart as the British. Himmler then wanted to inspect the Fort to see how Felix had managed to escape. He eventually left the Fort a very unhappy man. One up to us! All the preparation cleaning etc. had all been worth while as once again we had beaten the square heads.

At this stage I should mention that Scarface had got us a radio and we did manage to get scraps of news from varying sources via the radio which was at times a very tempremental piece of equipment. We did have regular searches through the Fort by various members of the Third Reich to try and find out about Felix's escape and what we knew about the escape, and if we gave a sarcastic remark in reply, like the British were accustomed to do to the Jerries, this landed us up with a week in the 'bunker'. These were small cells at the bottom of the Fort moat (it was a dry moat) and were not at all pleasant. One of these cells still has my writing on its walls which reads 'Give them bloody hell Winston' I have seen this recently on a video recording of the P.O.W. Forts and I recognised it instantly (Winston meaning Winston Churchill). I had a couple of sessions in there, the food whilst in the bunker, consisted of two slices of black bread and a half litre of water per day. No Red Cross food at all. No washing, no shaving, no books – just plain solitary. If they got too crowded they put two in a cell. It was on one of these bunker weeks that I met Jim Barber, who was later to be a very good friend. He had told one of the Jerries who questioned him about Felix's escape to 'piss off you little square head' and he joined me in a week's solitary.

A further contingent of the SS came to the camp whilst we were out at work one day and went through the Fort with a fine tooth comb. They found our radio. There was hell on. The Officers, including Padre Wild, were put into the bunkers and Scarface was taken away. None of the guards would talk about Scarface, and when we asked about him, we were strongly advised to leave the subject alone as this was Gestapo business with the Vermacht. Even though Scarface was a Jerry, we did feel rather bad about the way he had been treated, but we heeded the advice given and let the subject rest. We learned that he had been given a very quick trial and then shot.

From then on life got pretty grim. The theatre was shut down and the doors were boarded up, we had no means of any form of entertainment at all and the working hours were increased from nine hours per day to ten and a half hours. The Red Cross parcels became fewer and we were told that they could not get through because of British bombings. We started to get rather desperate, without the Red Cross parcels we were in trouble.

The Colonel brought out the rule that when the parcels arrived, instead of receiving one parcel each, we would have one between two people, thus building up a stock of food for emergencies. This did work and tins of stew were given to the kitchen and thus went a lot further.

CHAPTER NINE

Kartoffels and Black Shirts

A FTER the killing of Scarface, we were introduced to the new Commandant who was a right Nazi. He didn't want to know about our theatre, or Red Cross, he was immune to bartering and life got very strict with this gentleman. He told us that anyone caught escaping would be shot on sight. When Colonel McKie told him that it was a soldier's duty to try, and escape and reminded him of the Geneva Convention, he received a seven day spell in the bunker and was told to complain to his Geneva Convention.

The Commandant (who's name we never got to know) decided that we had too much of a cosy existence at the Fort, so he applied to the Vermacht to have us all split into working parties at various places, as he thought that too many Englanders together was not a good thing. Eventually, we were sent to different farms, building sites, on railway work, or such. I ended up on a farm with twenty other British lads including my pal Jim Barber. It was in the middle of February that the move was made and we had to walk all the way to a place called Zempleburg. The going was bad and the weather was bitterly cold with powdery snow about a foot thick. We walked all day, many of the lads getting very ill with the effects of the weather. We arrived at the farm on the outskirts of Zempleburg to find that we had a converted shed to sleep in, this was great after spending two nights in fields. The next week was spent making wooden beds, tables, forms to sit on and generally making it as best as we could. There was a Polish cook (who didn't have a clue what to cook apart from potato stew) and we gathered that the farm was now the property of a Baron (German) who had a daughter who ran the farm. Her name was Frauline Helga. She had a face like the back of a bus, a voice like a fog horn and a back-side like the side of a hill. She was a right Frauline!

Our first task was to top up the sauercraut barrels, the Jerries made their own sauercraut with cabbage, brine, salt and then sold the finished product at the market. We most certainly did fill them up with the best British salty urine that we could muster...I bet they tasted good!

We complained about the awful cooking which this daft Polish woman produced and as it was not yet fit to go on the land (the ground was still frozen), the Jerries let me cook the food with the help of this Polish lady for the camp. We pooled all our Red Cross food and I concocted some quite good meals, much to the amazement of the Polish lady. My pal Jim managed to get some white flour and believe it or not one day we had small meat and potato pies. The Poles thought we were mad as they had never seen stew with a crust on top.

We also managed to nobble the odd chicken or two which made a good stew, but we had to share it with the guards in case they told Helga. Burning the feathers was a problem because they smelled so much, but we managed.

Spring eventually came, and we had to work in the fields 'steinersamling' that is, picking up stones and carting them off the fields. I would mention at this stage that the soil in Poland was just sand and stones and I don't think that it has ever seen fertiliser or manure. We had to plough the fields with oxen – what stupid beasts they were. They knew the time better than we did. When it was six o'clock each day the stupid animals would just turn, wherever they were and head for the oxen sheds. The Jerries accepted this and allowed us to knock off at six.

The fields were planted with potatoes, rye and for Helga's personal use, a little wheat for white flour. I remember the harvest that particular year – the Jerries said it had been a good one. We had all the crops in the barn and Jim asked the guard if he could go to the toilet behind the barn, he seemed to be along time but no one really took much notice. We were all marched back to the farm at six. I asked Jim what the hell he had been upto and he replied you'll see – these bastards are not having this lot' (meaning the barn full of rye etc). About eleven o'clock (two hours after we had been locked up for the night) – the barn was on fire! The local fire brigade came and looked like something out of a comic strip. They could not get any water, so we had to pass water in buckets from the pond. The entire harvest was lost. I asked Jim what he had done as I knew he had had something to do with it. It appears, when he went for his 'scheisse' just before we returned to camp, he had climbed to the top of the crops inside the barn, hollowed out a part and lit a candle. When the candle burned down, it caught fire to the straw. The Jerries knew it was us that had caused the fire but we said how could we? We were locked up for two hours before the fire started. One Jerry said in all sincerity 'why don't you Englanders go back to England and leave us alone?' We smiled.

Autumn brought the harvest of kartoffels (potatoes) and all the small Polish children for miles around were rounded up and brought to the farm to gather the potatoes. A Polish child could be playing in the street and a German lorry would come along without any warning, take the kids to the farm where they would be threatened that if they escaped, misbehaved or did not work hard, their parents would be shot. About forty children aged between seven and twelve worked on the farm during the six week harvest. Although they were very weak they worked hard and adapted well. At times a child would cry for his family and home. Which usually had the effect of setting all the children off crying. This was very disturbing and reinforced our hate for the Nazis.

At this stage I was now a full time cook, having to feed the kids, look after any medical needs etc. Quite often I would have to put a stitch into some youngsters leg or hand and my cook house gradually became known as the Kranken Hauser (hospital)...some hospital...I had half a dozen well worn bandages a few rags for dressings, which I constantly boiled to keep reasonably sterile, a few precious aspirins and salt water as a disinfectant (not the kind used in Helgas sauercraut). The kids were not treated very well and the Black Shirts found a lot of pleasure in giving any child a beating. The black shirted yobs were about 19-20 years old...very much Hitler Youth trained and hated the world in general outside the Third Reich. We detested them. Even our guards would have nothing to do with them. They were known as Hitler bully boys. One or two of them tried to trade with us for English cigarettes etc but none of the British soldiers would have anything to do with them. Some of the Poles were not so good however, and turned Angi-deutch (which meant that they helped the Jerries) and these Poles were despised by both us, the majority of the Polish community and, I might add, the Germans too.

Not a lot happened at Zempleburg other than the daily routine of starting work in the fields at seven a.m. and returning to the farm at five in the afternoon. The children were housed in a barn a few hundred yards away from us, surrounded by barbed wire and a Polish lady cooked for them, although I believe that the main diet consisted of potatoes and rye soup. Breakfast consisted of a sort of porridge made of rye flour which was not too bad, but no-one ever put on weight and again I shudder to think what would have happened to us if it were not for the Red Cross parcels which arrived reasonably regularly. We once received an Australian Red Cross parcel which contained a lot of fancy things such as tinned fruit etc. which made a very nice change from the basic things inside the British Red Cross parcels...the Canadian parcels were excellent, but we had to share them between two people. On the farm we pooled all the tins of meat etc. as they went a lot further.

The Black Shirts (S.S.) guards over the kids did not like the look of our Red Cross parcels and tried to make life hard for us, although in fact, they had no right to interfere with us at all, but our guards were very frightened of them and kept a low profile.

CHAPTER TEN

Battling in the cookhouse

MY pal Jim, was working in the fields one day and I was busy getting the dinner ready for all the British, when he walked into the cook house with a Polish boy aged about twelve who had a very nasty looking cut above his eye-brow. He asked me if I could do anything, to which I replied that I would have to put a couple of stitches in as it was quite a gaping wound. I asked how the lad got such an injury and Jim told me that one of the S.S. had hit him because he was sky-larking with one of the other children. We sat the youngster down and with the barest of medication (the salt water to clean up) I managed to put a couple of stitches in, which held the wound together. We had no sticking plaster so it was a case of hoping that it would heal and not get infected. I told the lad to lie down with his head back and at that moment this bully boy with his black shirt bounced into the cook house asking were the young lad was and why he was not working. Jim said to him in perfect German...'Are you the one that did this to the little lad?' the Jerry answered 'Ja . What has it got to do with you?' to which Jim replied 'well let's see what you can do with an effing Englishman'. With that, Jim lashed out a purler, hitting the Jerry right between the eyes. Believe me, I never wanted to be at the receiving end of such a punch. He knocked the Jerry right through the cook-house door, breaking the door off its hinges, saying 'come on bastard, get up, you are good with kids, see if you can do the same with Englishmen.' The Jerry laid where he was, wiping blood away from his face and he blew a loud whistle, which brought another Black Shirt shouting Was ist loos (what is wrong). The second one saw the situation and set upon me, where I think that I put up a reasonable show. The years of humiliation from these German bastards brought out all the pent up anger in me and I laid into this Jerry with all the strength I could muster. The fact that he was a Jerry Black Shirt was bad enough, but the knowledge that he had ill treated these Polish children gave me even greater strength, and I was certainly going to see that he knew that he could not get away with this sort of treatment to children whilst British soldiers were around. I used my knees, my fists, my boots, and even head butted him which brought blood from his mouth. My face was battered, I was kicked, clawed and knocked nearly senseless, but this was my battle, my war, my very own enemy. This was the reason for me being in this dreadful war...His black shirt and his embroided swastika brought out some sort of animal fury that I had never known before and I fought him with every ounce of strength in my body. I wept with the frustration of not being able to beat this blackshirted bastard. If I could have mustered the strength, I know that I would have killed him with my bare hands. Jim, in the meantime was having his own private battle with Jerry number one.

The polish women were hysterical saying the Germans would kill us...eventually, Jim and I were overpowered by half a dozen black shirted S.S. and put in chains and taken to a very small shed with no light, no window, very little air. We were chained to a post and left without any food or water for three days. We had to do our toilet where we laid and although there was no light for us to see, I am sure that there were rats to keep us company. The Black Shirts would come in each morning presumably to see if we were still alive and delighted in telling us that we would get no Red Cross parcels anymore. They marched the Polish children by the shed everyday to see their 'English heroes', which both depressed the kids and did nothing to help our plight.

After three days the Gestapo arrived. We were unchained and let out into the blinding sun and questioned. We asked for water and were told that we could have water after we had answered the questions. Why had we attacked the German who was doing his duty for the Third Reich? Were we connected with the underground or the Polish resistance? I asked 'what bloody resistance?' (or words to that effect) for which I received an almighty belt across the face. I decided to keep quiet after that. We eventually got water and was told that we would receive a Court Martial for the offence. This would lead to punishment in a labour camp. We demanded to see a British Officer, which was refused.

A week later we were told that we were to be taken to Danzig (now known as Gdansk) for the Court Martial and although we could not have a British Officer to help us we could have a German Lawyer which would be paid for by the Red Cross. We had to sign a form to say that we would accept the services of the German Lawyer and agreed that the costs would be sent to the Red Cross who would pass them on to the British Government. We also agreed that a full report of the Court Martial would be sent to the Red Cross and on to the British Government.

CHAPTER ELEVEN

The Trial

THE day arrived before the day of the trial and we were put on a train with a very elderly guard (who was utterly fed up with Mr. Hitler and the war). We arrived in Danzig the next morning and were taken to the Court house. The trial was to start at 10.00 a.m. No lawyer! The Germans were adamant that the trial began so we were ushered into the court bedecked with swastikas and a photo of Hitler above the bench. All the Jerries saluted in the usual way, the right arm, and we were told to do like wise. Jim told them to urinate off. I also refused in like wise language. The trial started and the prosecutor made out that we were trying to start our own private war, trying to destroy the morale of the German army, by flaunting our Red Cross food and attacking the young innocent German S.S. who were only doing their duty and helping the young Poles.

At this moment the court door opened and a weird looking individual came in and announced that he was the lawyer sent to represent us. Jim said 'don't you mean defend us?' to which our lawyer replied 'no, you are already guilty'. I said 'Christ what sort of a trial is this going to be?' The court allowed us five minutes with this lawyer to state our case. It was hopeless, he was anti-British. We decided (Jim and I) that when we got back to court we would ask if we could defend ourselves without this lawyer.

When we went back into the court, this lawyer started his speech, not knowing that we both spoke perfect German and Jim interrupted him and asked the judges if we could defend ourselves as we did not consider it fair, us being British and the lawyer being German.

Eventually, after much discussion we were told we could defend ourselves providing that we signed a paper to say that we wished to dispense with the German lawyer's services and that he would be paid by the British Red Cross. We signed. We were asked if we needed an interpreter. We declined, saying that we knew the German language quite well. This seemed to please the judges, who wanted to know if we had learned German at school. We told him that we had learned German during the past four years in the German prison camps as an effort to survive and not through any affection for Germany. (We must have been seen as a pair of clever sods, but we were only trying to show that we were not afraid, although inwardly I was messing myself).

The trial started by the prosecution asking the judges to impose the death sentence as we had attacked the glorious members of the German S.S. I promptly asked what right he had to ask for a sentence when the trial had not even started? I was told in no uncertain terms that the German laws were different to the English law, whereas in Germany a person was automatically guilty until he proved his innocence and as this was a Military Court Martial, the rules of the Vermacht applied and accordingly, if the court so wished, the death sentence could be imposed and carried out, should the court find us guilty. I argued that this seemed a funny sort of law presuming everyone to be guilty before being heard. I was told that in my own interest I would be wise to be quiet and let the court proceed and pronounce its findings at the end of the trial. Jim (who was beside me) advised me to shut up, so the trial began.

The judges consisted of a Feldfebbel (Major) from the army, a senior officer from the German navy and a senior officer from the Luftwaffe (airforce) plus an interpreter, which we did not need.

The two S.S. youths were brought in (who we had belted, it came out that the one Jim had belted, suffered a fractured jaw and was missing three teeth) and said that we had made an attack on them whilst they were carrying out their duties and that all the British soldiers kept taunting the Germans with our Red Cross food, cigarettes and the British prevented them in doing their duties in looking after the young Polish children who were working for the glorious Third Reich.

We were allowed to ask them questions and they denied ever hitting the children and said that this particular child had fallen on a stone cutting his head because he was playing around with the other children. I asked the court if they believed a small child could possibly fall onto a stone and receive a cut which required two stitches? I was told that it could be possible.

Q. Why had we attacked the two S.S. men?

A. Because as British soldiers we wished to defend the Polish Children who had been taken from their homes and bullied by these S.S. guards.

Q. What right had we, as British Prisoners of war to attack the German S.S., regardless of why?

A. We believe in looking after children in Britain and not taking them from their homes.

The Germans responded by saying that these children volunteered for this work, and treated it as a country holiday and the S.S. were there purely to look after them and see that no danger came to them, especially from British P.O.W. who are renowned for causing as much trouble as possible.

The rest of the morning was spent arguing, but our case was

a hopeless one and was even turning political. We were (in the German eyes) interfering with the policies as laid down by the Third Reich, to do with other countries which their Fuhrer was now looking after.

Jim, my pal gave a good speech reminding the court of the Geneva Convention and the fact that their Fuhrer had nothing to do with us and that our Fuhrer was called Winston Churchill and our Fuhrer stood for freedom. I whispered to Jim to belt up as I feared that we were getting the judges backs up.

We were told that the court would adjourn for lunch and would announce its verdict at 2.00 p.m. Then came the daft thing. The court officials all went out and we were left with our pathetic little guard (he must have been about sixty years old). I asked him what we were going to do for the next two hours and he did not know, so he went and found a court official who told him to take us down the road to the cafe and give us something to eat. He gave him a chitty to present to the cafe which would cover expenses. So away we trotted to this cafe, the guard presented his chitty and we had a meagre lunch consisting of potato soup, black bread and coffee. This was ridiculous.

It was even more ridiculous when our poor old guard asked us if we would look after his rifle whilst he went to the toilet, and it must have looked a rather comic sight to see a couple of British Prisoners of War holding a German's rifle whilst he went to the toilet.

We chatted with this poor old man, who I think was terrified of us and only wanted to get back to his wife and children...he came from a small village just outside Hamburg. After the meal, we had a look round Danzig, which did not really impress us in the least and Jim and I talked about what we would do after the verdict was announced. We knew that it would be guilty, so the obvious thing was to make a run for it. Like bloody fools we did not run for it there and then in case our poor little guard would be in trouble even though we had every chance of making a break for it...its true what the Jerries kept saying, the English are mad.

We duly returned to the court and at 2.00 p.m. the court assembled and the prosecutor made his speech, saying that these two Englanders were making a mockery out of German justice; they had no respect for our Fuhrer and that he insisted on the death sentence.

The army Officer got up and said that the court had heard the case and considered that we had made a deliberate attack on these two fine young German S.S. soldiers, who were only doing their duty and as such we were guilty. Jim Barber was sentenced to one year in the Straffe Lager (hard labour camp) and I was also given the same sentence. We would receive no Red Cross food and no communication would be allowed with the Red Cross during the year of hard labour. This sentence would be notified to the Red Cross and would be confirmed from Berlin. In the meantime, we would be returned to the Fort and kept to await the sentence being confirmed.

So the 'trial' was over and we were on our way back to the Fort and the dungeons. We decided that we must escape as even if we were shot it would be better than a lingering death in the concentration camp as we could never last out a year without the Red Cross food.

CHAPTER TWELVE

The Thorn-Bromberg Road

WE were put into a dungeon in the fort and considered ourselves lucky as we were both in the same dungeon and so could make various plans. The lads in the Fort managed to smuggle Red Cross food in to us and to bribe the guards to let us have a good stock of food, ready for an escape.

The Jerries had got the breeze up over something or other and told us that we must be prepared to leave within ten minutes as the Russians are advancing and getting quite close to the Fort. Naturally, we were quite pleased about this as we had visions of the Russians taking us and repatriating us...it seems too good to be true. How the hell were we going to get out of the bloody dungeon though?

Our prayers were once again answered, one of the lads, a Corporal in the Green Howards, had bribed one of the guards with 500 cigarettes to let us out, so we mingled with the rest of the British lads all ready to evacuate the Fort.

Civilians were passing all the time ladden with bedding etc. all along the Thorn-Bromberg Road, so we knew that something was definitely happening. The guards had forgotten all about us and we mixed very freely with all the rest of the lads.

Today is January 20th and we have been called to prepare to evacuate. We were allowed to go to another Fort which was about 100 yards away and get as much Red Cross food as we could carry, providing that we shared it with the German

Picture of Fort 13, Thorn, Poland.

guards. Our officers agreed to this so all the British obtained as much food as they could carry. Jim and I managed to cram the contents of five parcels into our kit bags taking the most valuable survival goods only, and not bothering about such items as soap etc.

At 9.00 a.m. we started the march which was to be a survival march, through atrocious weather...the snow was about a foot deep. As night fell we were ushered into a field and told that we would be moving on when the dawn broke. We made fires out of what wood was available, the Jerries helping and we made tea from melted snow and ice. The guards knew that the Russians were advancing and kept telling us how good they had been to us British and that they had not volunteered for the War and would we tell the Russians how good they had been to us. We were elated, they were terrified.

The next day at dawn, we started marching in the Bromberg direction. At a certain cross-roads we met other P.O.W.'s from other camps all who were being evacuated from the area. As we waited, about 400 Jewesses passed us, begging for food or clothing. We gave them what we could spare, trying to avoid the Gestapo's eyes as if they caught us giving these girls anything they beat them with very large sticks. We gave one girl who looked very ill some of our black bread and a few marmite cubes, but one of the S.S. guards saw her take it from us and smashed her head in. She was dead within seconds. I wanted to have a go at this bastard, but the rest of the lads pointed out the futility of a fight with these Jerries, who were armed and would quite happily kill the lot of us.

That night we were once again ushered into the fields of deep snow, again the fires and no sleep at all. About 11.00 p.m. one of the lads, a youngster called Adams, was taken ill. He had pains in this stomach, a dreadful cough and he looked awful. We learned that there was a British Medical Officer in the field, so he was brought to young Adams, but said there was nothing possible that we could do for him except keep him as warm as possible. He thought he had pneumonia. We did our best with the Jerries helping, giving him cocoa every hour to keep him warm. It was a hopeless task, with the bitterly cold temperature.

Sunday 21st January – We started marching again at 6.00 a.m. dragging young Adams on a rough sledge covered with our overcoats (we took it in turns to lend our coats as it was so cold, we could not last without a coat for over an hour.

The going was bad, very bad, and nearly creased us as our packs were so heavy with the tins of Red Cross food that we had brought with us. We came to the town of Schulitz where we found a small band of British P.O.W's who were staying on until the Russians came and they promised to look after young Adams, so we carried on leaving him in good hands. With our burden taken off our hands, the going was a little better. Jim and I decided that today we MUST make our escape, as we knew that our number would be up if the Jerry Officers found out who we were (convicted to the Labour camps). The main object was to get rid of the two guards who were with our sections. They were very tired, fed up, and not taking an awful lot of notice of us. The moment came when both the guards decided to have a wee. We ran and ran until we came to a deserted farm about 200 yards from the road and from an upstairs window in this farm, we watched the column walk by. We felt that we were pretty safe for a while.

We made a pot of tea and had a meal out of black bread and a small tin of Red Cross salmon. Such luxury. We had a well needed wash, we could hear heavy gun-fire in the distance and knew that 'Joe' was not far away. (We called the Russians Joe because of Joe Stalin). During our meal a German Soldier wandered into the farm, stood to attention and saluted us and asked if he could stay for a while as he had deserted the army and was fed up with the war and Hitler.

He had no weapons only pictures of his wife and kids. We gave him a cup of tea and let him stay. We felt good. Here was a Jerry asking if he could stay, with us...a right turn up for the books! This Jerry told us that we must not stay as if we were caught, we would be shot on sight by the Gestapo who were at the end of the column of marchers. The Jerry told us that our best bet was to try and get to Bromberg, as the Germans had evacuated Bromberg and it would be the first to fall into Russian hands. We decided to risk it and stayed the night at this farm, no lights at all but at least we were out of the atrocious weather and reasonably warm.

At dawn, we found our German friend had vanished leaving a scribbled note saying 'Danke Englanders Gutten Gluck' (thanks Englishmen good luck) so we thought it was best to take his advice and make for Bromberg. We saw a long trail of civvies and we managed to hang on to a wagon which pulled us along the ice covered roads until we reached the outskirts of Bromberg.

We saw a typical Polish house and decided to ask for help. Our luck was in, the Poles were friendly and agreed to hide us. I had my doubts about them I must confess, as they spoke perfect German, but they assured us that they would look after us and gave us a small, hidden room adjoining the cow shed. It appeared that every Polish house had a hidden room somewhere in the house. In the room was a small, but adequate bed and chair. A tiny window let in the light. Jim slept in the bed and I slept on the floor and it was like a hotel.

CHAPTER THIRTEEN

Polish hospitality at Bromberg

THE following day, the Polish lady woke us up, and assured us that it was safe and she took us into the house where she made us a breakfast of milk soup and fried sliced potatoes. We offered them coffee but they dare not take it as making coffee would send out an aroma which any passing German might detect. We had tea instead.

They had a radio and we desperately tried to get any sort of news, but failed. We stayed in the house about two hours and watched Englishmen going by in two's and three's with no guards in sight, all obviously making for Bromberg. We gave the lady two tins of Red Cross meat and she made a very good soup, by adding peas and potatoes. We then went back to our hidden room.

At 4.00 p.m. we heard a commotion in the yard and saw through the tiny window a bunch of Germans arguing with the Polish lady. This made us very uneasy. About half an hour later she came to our hidden room to say that we must go as soon as it was dark as her home and farm were to be the German H.Q. This area was now the front line against the advancing Russians. I felt my heart in my throat, because if we were found, we would be shot without hesitation.

We managed to creep out of the hide-away when it got dark with no-one seeing us and made our way to Bromberg. No Jerries at all. The place looked empty. We came across a friendly Pole who assured us that he liked all Englishmen (funny how these Poles all spoke perfect German) and we could stay at his house. We had by now picked up another British lad who was on his own. We all had a conference and decided to stay there until the Russians came...there were us three, the Polish man and wife, their 18 year old daughter and a 15 year old son. They were all terrified of the advancing Russians and seemed to fear them more than they feared the Germans. We could not understand why, but we were surely going to find out. We had enough Red Cross food to last us about a fortnight, if we were careful. The Poles had nothing, they had even eaten their bloody chickens. It was now 11.00 p.m. Gunfire and machine gun fire could be heard quite plainly. We estimated that the Russians would be with us by the morning. We decided to take it in turns to have a sleep. The bed was down stairs so we had two hours each, two sharing the bed. The girl (Regina) was terrified and cried all the night. Her father told us that the Russians raped all girls. Poor sods, they were very frightened. By 1.00 a.m. (Tuesday 23rd) 3 others went to bed.

It is 3.00 a.m. I have just made a pot of tea and feel better for it. There is merry hell going on outside. Heavy gunfire and terrific explosions, two of these explosions have extinguished our carbide lamp. The whole building shakes. Up to now, we have not heard any 'air' activity. Heavy transport can be heard moving, but we do not know if it is German or Russian. By now the explosions are so bad no one attempts to sleep. We are all in excellent spirits hoping to meet our Russian allies very soon.

3.10 a.m. A woman neighbour burst in to say the tanks are now coming. The gunfire has stopped. The Pole decides that he will go out to see what is happening.

3.50 a.m. The Pole returns and says that there are no tanks in the city but they can be heard quite plainly massing at the outskirts of Bromberg. We expect that they will take the city at dawn. It is 17 degrees of frost outside.

4.30 a.m. No change. Everything is still and there is a great tension in the air. The expectancy makes our nerves on edge, coupled with Regina's continuous crying.

6.30 a.m. I have made a make-shift breakfast of Red Cross porridge and tea and we all have our fill.

7.00 a.m. The firing has started again but seems to be out-flanking Bromberg, there is no sign of any tanks...can't quite make this out.

8.30 a.m. Regina has just gone into Bromberg to try and barter a tin of cocoa for some bread (which is very scarce). Everything is deadly quiet except for the occasional burst of distant gunfire. There is something very funny going on and I am not at all happy with the situation.

During the morning many Poles came in and chatted to us...all thinking that the Russian army had by-passed Bromberg on its way to Berlin. Pity, we had hoped to have met our Russian friends and be on our way home. (How daft can you get?).

I made a dinner consisting of mashed potatoes and meat gravy (thanks once again to the Red Cross). During the dinner a Pole came in and told us that there were some more Englishmen just down the road. We asked him if there were any Jerries about and he assured us that everything was clear, so we decided to pay these lads a visit to see if we could cadge a few fags from them as our supply had by now run out.

CHAPTER FOURTEEN

Crossfire and vodka

T HERE was no firing in progress and all seemed quite peaceful and we thought that a stroll would do us good. We walked down the road about 200 yards when a very frightened German appeared and said 'Gutten Tag' (good morning) and he was on his way. (What sort of bloody war is this?) Then a lot of firing started near to us (too close for our liking) so we thought that our best plan would be to get back to the house, as we could see no signs of any other Englishmen.

Then the firing really did start. We dived under cover of a tree and a burst from a machine gun rattled angrily over our heads. We talked it over and came to the conclusion that we were out walking on the actual road under fire from both sides. The Jerries were on one side and the Russians on the other, with us three idiots slap bang in the middle. We ran from tree to tree with bullets and shells flying all around us. Everytime we broke cover of a tree, a Russian machine gun fired at us. Then we took cover from the machine gun, the bloody Jerries had a go at us from their side. Finally, running from tree to tree and eventually crawling along a ditch we managed to reach a house. A German soldier lay outside with a very nasty bullet wound in his arm. I bound him up as best as I could with his field dressing (he could not understand why an Englishman was helping him) and he went on his way. By this time Dunkirk hadn't a look in. We dived into the house and into the cellar where a lot of civvies were hiding.

Five minutes passed with really heavy firing, then the door of the cellar burst open and half a dozen Russians came in and ordered us out. We were terrified. Then came the task of convincing them that we were British. One of the Russians spoke German so we tried to tell him who we were (in German) and that we were escaped P.O.W.s. He wanted to know why we spoke German and not English? We realised by speaking German we had made an awful mistake. They held a little conference and kept looking very angry at us.

Then they told us to stand against the wall. I said to Jim this is where we get the bullet....Jim replied saying 'looks like it', but we decided to have another go this time in English. We pattered on about how we had waited five long years for the wonderful Russian army to come along and free us from the Germans. This seemed to create a bit of doubt and they asked us if we had any papers to prove that we were British. We showed them our P O.W. discs round our necks and by sheer luck, Jim had his old army pay book on him. This seemed to convince them a bit more and we made gestures with Stalin and Churchill shaking hands.

One Russian with a tommy gun was chosen and we were told to march with our arms out-spread. He took us across a field about two feet deep in snow and then through some small streets were we encountered a gang of Russians stinking of vodka. They dived into our pockets, ripping our jackets open asking for watches or rings. We had none. They were like animals and I realised why little Regina was so terrified at the thought of meeting them.

We were put in a room with two German prisoners, who had been badly beaten up. Finally, we were taken to another house where the Russian flag was flying and we met our first Russian Officer...A WOMAN. Imagine our surprise when she stepped out of this massive tank carrying a tommy gun under her arm. She said Ah Anglichanis (words which we never forgot meaning English). She took us to see the commanding officer, which turned out to be Field Marshall Zhukov. He spoke a bit of English and we managed to convince him that we were in fact British soldiers, escaping from the Germans. He shook hands with us, gave us a drink of fiery vodka and a pack of Russian cigarettes. He asked us to point out the German positions, which we did to the best of our ability and he said within a week you will be back in England. To the Germans he said, within a week Siberia. As we were about to leave (God knows where we were going) a further five battle dresses appeared down the street. We were told to wait for them. They turned out to be 5 Cypriots so we were both able to identify each other as British subjects.

Marshall Zhukov took great delight in cutting the P.O.W. discs from round our necks and throwing them in the fire...more vodka...I was gradually liking the Russians more and more...More vodka...I was gradually getting pissed! I do not remember much more about that day, all I know is that I woke up with a very thick head and tongue which felt like sand paper. I declined further vodka.

A Russian escort was given to us to act as a guide and interpreter (we were warned that it would be dangerous for us to travel alone) and he was to show us the way to the Russian H.Q. When we arrived we were thoroughly searched and told that we would be warm that night. (The cold was unbelievable). We were ushered into a pig sty with four or five pigs to sleep. It stank, but we were warm. It was a very uncomfortable night as the bloody pigs kept snorting in our ears.

On Wednesday 24th we started to walk with our Russian

escort (we could not find out his name, so we called him Ivan the Terrible) to a place called Alexandrova which had been set up as a receiving camp for P.O.W's etc. Polish and Russians gave us sweets, cigars, meat and sugar. We were told to go to any deserted farm and kill any animal for meat if we wanted anything. All the land now belonged to Russia and the Anglichanis are Russia's best friends with Veenston Chochell dobra Anglichani, (Winston Churchill a good Englishman). We learned a few words of Russian, just enough to show them that we were friendly...they did not seem to like the Americans or Americanskis as they used to say. The argument was that the Americans waited until the English and the Russians had nearly won the war before coming in. They mentioned that the Russians had lost millions of soldiers at Stalingrad, as we did not know much about the politics of the war, we decided to stay out of that argument.

We did not make Alexandrova that day, but we passed hundreds of tanks. Yanky lorries full of Russians, armoured wagons and the famous cossacks. They rode very sturdy small horses and wore padded hats as opposed to the normal khaki Russian hats. As soon as they knew that we were English it was all smiles, out came the vodka, big hand shakes, cigarettes and meat.

At about 5.00p.m. it was getting dark so we picked out a deserted farm to spend the night. One of the Cypriots killed a calf, a pig, 4 chickens, a rabbit and a pigeon. We kept the fur from the rabbit and Jim and I made good face protection from the bitter cold.

We cooked the lot in a sort of boiler and had a really good meal leaving enough for further meals the next day. What an International crowd we were. During the meal, two Russian

Officers came in and joined us...no red tape here...so the party was made up of two Russian officers, our Russian guide, 5 Cypriots, 1 Pole and 1 Czechoslovakian. In our various languages we all came to the same conclusion that the War had gone on too long and that there is too much red tape in the British Army in comparison with the Russians. We had a splendid time with these two officers, but I had a job explaining to them why I am writing all this down as they don't seem to have heard of diaries. We have to speak in a mixture of languages and signs, but we managed.

CHAPTER FIFTEEN

The cold road to Alexandrova

THURSDAY 25th. We woke up at about 5.00 a.m. after a good nights sleep to find that the Cypriot cook had hot tea waiting for us. Unfortunately, there was no bread but there was plenty of meat so we had our fill (have you ever had stew for your breakfast at 5.00 a.m. in the morning). We left the remainder of the meat outside and it soon froze, ready to go in our packs for the rest of the journey.

We arrived at Argenau around noon. All along the way, we were challenged by the Russians and when our guide told them that we were Anglichanis, we had outstretched hands, masses of smiles and we felt as though we were amongst friends. Many times we were very glad that we had our Ivan, the interpreter, to explain who we were.

We had a fantastic reception at Argenau. First we were taken to the Polish H.Q. where we were given a very good meal and cigarettes. All the Poles and Russians were very glad to see us. They gave us a good billet with 5 French civvies then the Russians and Poles brought us rations which consisted of a loaf of bread each, about 5lb of fat pork between us and a pot of jam. We felt secure and warm.

We were told to have our evening meal at the central dining hall, specially for ex-P.O.W.'s and refugees. These meals consisted of barley and potato soup with a little meat. A Polish town government had been set up and they seemed to be getting things organised. We were told by the Polish officials that we should probably have to wait a few days for transport to Alexandrova which was 25 kilometers away. They said that the road from Argenau was not safe as there were parties of Germans still there ready to shoot on sight.

Friday 26th still saw us at Argenau. We had made no further arrangements for travelling as the roads were too deep in snow, not to mention the bitterly freezing weather and the reports of bands of Germans. We drew our daily rations and we were definitely OK for food. We were allowed to wander around the town just as we pleased and it was certainly good to know that there was no Jerry guard at our heels. All the Poles and Russians were very pleased to see us and kept wandering in to see the Anglichanis for themselves. I happened to mention to a Pole that I was a pianist and without any further hesitation, he took us to his house where he had a dilapidated old piano which had not seen a tuner since its birth, but I managed to knock a tune out of it, much to the delight of the entire Polish community. Jim got hooked up with a Polish girl called Elsa, (quite pretty) so that left Sid and myself to have a wander around the town.

As the weather had calmed down a bit, we were not wearing hats, hoping that the Russians would find us a couple of Russian hats, when a Polish official stopped us and asked us where our hats were. Hoping for the Russian type hats, we said we had none. We were taken to the Polish H.Q. given a meal then he took us outside, down some steps into a cellar where a sorry bunch of Germans were locked up. They were all civilians and very frightened. We were told to pick any hat as they would soon have no use for them. We refused the offer, which the Polish officer could not comprehend, nevertheless, it was a good feeling to be at the other side of the wire.

Saturday 27th. We decided to try and get to Alexandrova today, starting at 6.00 a.m. but the weather was so bad it made travelling impossible, however, at 9.00 a.m. the wind dropped so we said farewell to Argenau. This day proved to be the worst day for travelling as wind and snow nearly cut us to bits. We had to stop every half an hour or so to take shelter from the weather, as our eye lids frosted over and any part of us exposed to the weather was liable to severe frost bite, so we were very careful and took no chances. The travelling was awful, knee deep in powdery snow with a head wind. The weather was dreadful. Such bitter cold is never experienced in England.

About 2.00 p.m. we arrived at the village of Glasnau and a very gruesome sight awaited our arrival. As we entered the village four very dead Germans laid on the road side, frozen stiff, their boots had been taken off and they had obviously been stripped of any possessions. This was not a very cheerful greeting to us, even though they were Germans, as they must have laid there a week or more. Our little Russian guide, Ivan, made signs to indicate that these were good Germans, as all good Germans were dead ones. There was great evidence of fierce battles here as there were burned out tanks of both German and Russian origin all over the place. Most of the town was in ruins and most walls bore bullet or shell scars.

A young girl was walking towards us, so we stopped and explained that we were British soldiers and asked where we could obtain some food. She took us to a Red Cross Station (Polish Red Cross) and they gave us coffee and later soup. We were so exhausted that we asked if we could stay the night and they were delighted to put us up, so we stayed the night.

That night, we actually slept in a bed...absolute luxury. The Poles in this Red Cross Station were very friendly to us and wanted us to stay until the weather got better, but we thought it better to push on. You will note that I often say that the Poles in some instances were very friendly, well, I emphasise this as there were quite a lot of Poles that were distinctly unfriendly and were known as Angy-deutch (German collaborators). These were feared by everyone as they would go out of their way to assist the Germans (often in exchange for food etc.) Luckily these Angys were no longer around now, as most of them had been rounded up by the Poles or the Russians and shot.

On Sunday 28th, we moved off at 7.30 a.m. on what we hoped would be the last stretch to Alexandrova. The weather was still bitterly cold and the going was bad. All along the road sides were dead Germans, frozen stiff, all had their boots removed and it was obvious that their pockets had been rifled. The Russians had no respect for the live Germans and a lot less for the dead ones. Ivan hated the Jerries – dead or alive.

We passed parties of Russians, most of them drunk out of their minds, but in a rough sort of way, friendly to us Anglichanis. We stayed in a deserted farm over night, thawing out our meat and cooking it to make a stew of sorts. We survived.

The next day saw us setting off at the crack of dawn and after a dreadful day travelling in the most appalling weather, we reached Alexandrova at 10.30 a.m. The town had been badly devastated by both German and Russian artillery, but we managed to find a make-shift hospital where we stayed for an hour. They gave us hot coffee and bread. We were told to go a further 7 kilometers to a place called Hermansbad where there were a lot of British soldiers, who, like us, had escaped. After our rest, we got on our way, this time the going was not too bad, as the wind had dropped and the snow under-foot was hard packed with the traffic going over it. So we made good time today and arrived at Hermansbad at around 4.00 p.m. in the afternoon. The cold was so severe that there was never any slush, only hard packed ice.

CHAPTER SIXTEEN

That Glenn Miller fellow again!

The Hotel at Ciecocinek.

THE Russians showed us to a very big Hotel where we found British officers in command over 100 British. There was also a lot of French, Belgians, Australians and a scruffy bunch of Americans (the Yanks never washed or shaved and looked like a load of gypsies). Our officers told them to smarten themselves up, but they didn't want to know. Jim and I were given a very nice room and we soon had a good fire going, as the Angy-deutch Poles were made to chop wood all day long for our fires.

On Monday we were registered with the Russians. These Russians seemed to be a better breed than the ones we had encountered on the way here...more educated and very friendly. They told us that they would get us repatriated back to England as soon as possible. The food here was not good and consisted of a loaf of black bread between three, and a bowl of soup per day. We still considered ourselves lucky to be alive, so there were no grumbles...After all, the Russians had exactly the same as us.

We were allowed to go into the town as we wished, naturally complying with the Russian regulations (and the British Officers red tape).We had to be in an hour before dark etc. We had no money, not that it would have been any good as there was nothing to buy in the shops, but the black market flourished and such items as cigarettes, clothing etc. could be exchanged for rare items like eggs. Sid, I regret to admit, scrounged off our Russian hosts and flogged what we had to the ever ready black market receivers and so we existed.

This hotel was fantastic. There were two full sized grand pianos in it so I was well at home. We decided that we should have an international concert, so all nationalities got together and we had a wide range of entertainers from all countries. We had a concert that would have done the Palladium proud. There was a team of Russian Dancers who were absolutely fantastic...God knows where they got the energy from, and quite a lot of Russian singers. I did not know their music but followed along on the piano as best as I could. We had a French comedian and although we could not fully understand his jokes, one would gather that they were for a men-only audience! There were three Russians playing Balalikas and they were first class, playing music which I will remember all my life. The Russian music was all folk music and this was the first time that I was to hear Lyenka... fantastic! there was a very good Italian juggler who was almost a comedian in a funny sort of way. The Yanks just looked on, as scruffy as ever. One Yank came over to me at the piano and asked me if I knew any Glen Miller Music?

This rang a bell with me, so I asked this Yank who was Glen Miller? He told me he was a very big 20 piece band who played a new sounding music. This Yank (who appeared to have a minute sort of intelligence) told me about the new sound with a clarinet lead and mentioned a few of the numbers which we had discarded, such as Moonlight Serenade, In the Mood, and others. He described in a weird sort of way how they should be played and I realised that we had thrown away a fantastic library of the very latest music.

We had one particular concert one evening which I will always remember. It was mostly the Russians who entertained, but their dancing and acrobatics had to be seen to be believed. I played a good sing-a-long for our lads and the vodka flowed. How the hell these Russians drank so much, I will never know. We had a couple of glasses and started talking about our rich relations, whereas the Ruskies drunk it by the bottle...absolute fire water.

CHAPTER SEVENTEEN

Ten day journey to the
Odessa State Circus

ON the Monday, we were put in parties and told that we were going to be registered with the Russian Government. This was an experience. First we had to write our names and addresses (in English) plus our regiment, regimental number and P.O.W. number. Then this was all translated into Russian. I never knew that my name could look like it was in Russian. Each man took approximately one hour so you can gather that this was a very slow process.

The Russian Town Mayor gave us a speech which we gathered meant that now that we were all registered, arrangements would be made with MEESTER CHOCHEEL in England to have us repatriated as soon as possible. Unfortunately, no one knew quite how to get in touch with Meester Chocheel in England.

We stayed at this place for about a month, selling our extra clothes, blankets etc. to the Poles in exchange for food. We started a really good 'buy and sell' racket buying clothes etc. for fat, sugar etc. and then re-sold the clothes to the Poles for a very good profit. Thereby, we managed to live quite reasonably. After about a month of Hermanbadd (Polish Ciechocinek) three of us decided to hitch a lift into Thorun to see if we could pick up anything worth having. We set off at 8.00 a.m. and hitched a lift from some Ruskies. A friendly Polish farmer gave us some dinner (the usual potato soup). We stayed the night at a Polish Red Cross Hostel sleeping on straw mattresses on the floor.

Thorun had had a good bashing by the Russians and there was nothing left of our former Stalag and camps. The Russians had looted the lot, good and proper. There were many stories of Russian soldiers raping, looting and generally behaving like animals.

There were hundreds of Russian lorries going to Bromberg, so we decided to have a trip back there. We asked a Russian Captain if we could beg a lift. He put us in the back of the lorry with some Russian soldiers who treated us like royalty. They gave us cigarettes, bread, meat and the usual bottle of vodka.

We arrived at Bromberg at 3.00 p.m. in the afternoon to visit our former hide-outs. The first one was ransacked and deserted, but at the second one, the civvies who took us in were there and delighted to see us. We stayed the night, collected our kit which we had left (it was devoid of any Red Cross food). The next morning we got another Russian lorry to Thorun and another back to Hermansbadd. The journey had proved to be quite interesting as we had seen the 'free' Thorun and Bromberg, both badly battered – also thousands of lorries, armoured cars, tanks etc. going to the front.

We stayed at Ciechocinek for a further 5 weeks and on March 3rd at 11.30 a.m. we were put into lorries to take us to another destination for our eventual re-patriation. We arrived at the town of Wreshm at 10.15 a.m. having had no sleep at all during the night's journey as it was too cold. We were put into a huge camp with 4000 Froggies, Belgiums, Dutch and Ities. We were put into rooms, 22 to a small room. To sleep meant good packing, but we managed. During the night, there were four big air raids, the anti-aircraft guns kept us awake.

The next day at 11.30 a.m. we left Wreshm and marched to the station where we were put into big 50 ton railway trucks. There were 60 men to a truck, rather crowded, but again, we managed. We were supplied with two stoves per truck, lamps and straw mattresses. The food rations were very poor and sparse, but we honestly believe that the Russians gave us all that they could. The journey lasted 10 days...very monotonous being cramped up, but relieved with the occasional stop for us to answer the call of nature. It was interesting to see Poland, and eventually Russia and the vast Ukraine. The route we took was Wreshm, Kutno, Warsaw, Praga, Bolgni, Sedlic, Brestlitowck, Rowno, Kowel, Smelinka, Tiraspol, Odessa.

At our many stops we traded with the Russian peasants for roubles to buy eggs, bread, bits of sausage etc. The Russians saw that we received a daily ration of bread, water, cigarettes and fiery vodka. It was sad to see Warsaw the capital of Poland absolutely flattened as we passed through...the Poles in Warsaw looked very dejected and hopeless. God only knows how on earth they will re-build anything out of all this rubble, as there did not seem to be a building left.

We eventually arrived at Odessa where we were met by Russian representatives who gave us a good hot meal, a well needed bath and de-louse (we were crawling with lice) I never thought that I could ever appreciate a bath so much. We were also given brand new British army uniforms and boots...all the lousy clothes were burned. We were given 40 English cigarettes (oh boy they were good after smoking the very strong Russian fags). We also received two large bars of English chocolate and a large bar of soap. Then came British and American representatives to tell us that we would soon be on our way home. We were issued with 20 cigs and chocolate each day also Red Cross parcels. Tea was issued twice a day along with a good hot meal.

We were not allowed out of our billet in Odessa, although the Russians did treat us well, but it seemed, with a funny sort of caution. We never saw the British or the American delegates again, I gather that they had left Odessa to see to the other ex-P.O.W.'s. The place that we were in was a large building which looked as though it had not been used for years. It encircled a courtyard with trees etc. and I suppose it could have been quite pleasant in different circumstances.

Odessa had been badly bombed by the Germans and there were many unsafe looking buildings. One night, we learned that four Americans had been killed by a falling derelict building.

One Thursday, our hosts told us that our meal would be an hour early...we asked why, and were told that we would soon see. Sure enough, after our meal, we were told to put on our uniforms and parade in the courtyard. We were very mystified. Then in came a dozen or more vicious looking Russians with machine guns who in no uncertain manner ordered us out into the street. We were terrified, as although the Russians had so far been quite friendly, there was always that doubt in the back of one's mind as to what they would do next.

We went out into the street...20 of us...to find a Russian military band outside. We were told to fall in behind the band and we were marched through Odessa while the band played Roll out the Barrel. This carried on for over half an hour (can you imagine what it was like to have Roll out the Barrel played continuously for over half an hour) it was the only British tune that they knew. We came to the conclusion that this was a propaganda effort by the Russians, but NO. We eventually arrived at a sort of theatre, still with the armed guards with machine guns at their side. We were ushered into this theatre, taken upstairs into the circle to find that we were guests of honour at the Odessa State Circus. The audience applauded us as we sat down, with the armed guards keeping a very strict watch over us. (Funny way to enjoy a show!).

It was a good show indeed, no animals at all, but plenty of acrobats, trapeze artists and the fabulous Russian dancers. The show ended 10.00 p.m. and amid much applause, we went outside to find that the band were still there waiting for us and to play Roll out the Barrel all the way back to our Billet. Crazy!

I had learned quite a few words of Russian, such as Dobra Utro (good morning) Ya neponimyeo (I do not understand) Spaceeba (thank you) Herbates (tea) Dosvidanya (good bye), which always pleased the Ruskies. If you could just speak one or two words, they were delighted (and usually brought forward a packet of cigarettes, or Vodka). English men kept coming in dribs and drabs, the Russians having rounded them up and sent them on to Odessa, until there was about 30 of us.

CHAPTER EIGHTEEN

An orange for the journey home

EVENTUALLY the big day came. We were told that there was an English ship in the harbour and that arrangements were being made to send us home. This was very exciting for us, as we could hardly believe that freedom was so near at hand. We were told that it would be about a week before we would be sailing and during that week, the Russians went out of their way to be as helpful as possible. The Russian Officer in charge asked that we would say how well we had been treated in Russia when we got home. We were all given an orange each...something which we had not seen for five long years – and an absolute luxury in Russia. They were as sour as hell, but went down very well...I know that some of the lads even ate the skins as well.

The day before we were due to board the ship, we were given new British Uniforms (God knows where they had come from) and we spent the day cleaning and polishing boots etc. all ready for the big day. I do not think that many of us slept that night, at all.

7.00 a.m. Our Russian hosts came in to say that we would be leaving at 9.00 a.m. to see your Meester Chocheel and Anglichani, (Mr Churchill and England). I would add at this point that the Russians had the greatest respect for Winston Churchill and looked upon him as a God-like figure.

At 9.00 a.m. the Russian Officers came and shook hands with us all, saying Dosvidanya to us all in turn (good bye). We had a British Officer with us and he was kissed on both cheeks, much to his surprise. We learned that this was a mark of true friendship and respect.

So, outside we went to find the band all lined up and we had to march behind them right through Odessa with them playing the one and only tune, Roll out the Barrel. Christ, I never want to hear that tune again. The Russian civvies waved to us, some of them even threw the odd flower at us...we felt like heroes but can't think why?

We eventually arrived at the docks and there it was...a sight for our sore and weary eyes...A real British ship flying the red ensign. Tears came into all our eyes...we could not believe it was true.

All along the docks were British goods such as Tate & Lyle bags of sugar in large sacks...cases of corned beef (which I believe the Russians did not like) tanks and armoured cars from England and USA.

The Russian Officer gave us a speech (after he had stopped that bloody band playing Roll out the Barrel). It was in Russian and we could not understand a word of what he was saying, but he finished off by saying dosvidanya, which we knew meant goodbye so we all replied with dosvidanya y spacceba (thank you).

Another official started to call out our names and we then walked up the gangway into the ship, after giving our Army number. He had some very peculiar ways of pronouncing English names, but eventually came Veelums Erich, which I knew was me. I stepped forward and gave my Army number 4344725 and was told to pass. God, could it be true? The Captain greeted us and said 'Welcome back to England, as now that you are aboard this ship you are in British territory'.

There were Red Cross nurses who were angels themselves. They had come over on this ship to look after us on our homeward journey. We were told to go to the dining room where there was white bread on the table (presumably to have with soup) but the lot was scoffed within minutes... British bread tasted like cake to us after years of rye bread. When the cooks came with the soup, they could not understand where the bread had gone, until we told them we had eaten and enjoyed it so much. We had a real meal of potatoes, vegetables and meat, followed by ice cream and tea. What a feast. We had forgotten what ice cream looked like, let alone the taste of it.

That evening, amid much waving, we set sail from Odessa, with that band still playing its Roll out the sodding Barrel! We sailed across the Black Sea, through the Bosphorus and anchored off Istanbul. We were told that two more British ships would be joining us to make a convoy when we entered the Mediterranean. Istanbul looked fantastic and we could see the Blue Mosque, the Koptaki Palace, all the minarettes etc. What a pity that we were not allowed ashore. The shipping here was fantastic, with boats of every description weaving in and out of the harbour. That evening, we sailed again through Dardenells, into the Sea of Marmara and eventually into the Mediterranean. We went through the Greek archipelligo, a group of very pretty islands, and lazed about the decks getting a lot of sunshine and rest. The accommodation on the ship was sparse, but good. Hammocks had been made for us and after the first night, we found them very comfortable. The food was excellent and the Red Cross girls were always at hand to see that we ate well and were looked after.

When I think back, I really owe my very existence to the various countries' Red Cross Teams, as I am confident that without The Red Cross Organisations, there would be only a handful of us left to tell the tale. I vowed that I would never pass a Red Cross collecting box again without dropping in a donation.

We passed Sicily, went past Capri and sailed up to Naples where we were told that a further two ships would be joining our convoy, plus a couple of destroyers, as there were still a few German U boats in the Mediterranean. The order was no smoking after dark, no lights on deck and after dark, to be quiet as possible (no music etc). We left Naples, after having had much Italian ice cream, plus a visit from some Italian gentleman who gave us a speech in Italian, – which we could not understand! He had a Chain of Office around his neck and we gathered that he was the Mayor of Naples. Bless him...he did his best.

We sailed through the Mediterranean without incident for a couple of days, until all of a sudden, all hell was let loose. Two destroyers were racing round the convoy like nobody's business, making a 'whoop, whoop', with their sirens. We all came to a halt. We asked what was going on and were told that the destroyers had spotted a German submarine. They were shooting off the end of the destroyers what looked like small barrels...we learned that these were in fact depth charges. This went on for an hour or more and we never got to know whether they had got the submarine or not.

We sailed on, and eventually came to Gibraltar. What a fantastic rock Gibraltar is. Again, we were not allowed ashore but we could see the entire town of Gibraltar was a mass of Union Jacks. A wonderful sight. It was very sunny and life felt good.

Before leaving Gibraltar, we were told to wear our life jackets at all times as this was the dangerous leg of the journey. Again, no smoking on deck, no lights and be quiet at night. The journey passed without any further incident, although most of us (including the Red Cross girls) were very sea sick when we crossed the rough Bay of Biscay.

Eventually, we saw land on the right hand side of the ship. We asked if it was France and were told NO THAT'S ENGLAND. We were coming up the West Coast of England to a yet unknown landing destination. Most of us were in tears at the thought of ever seeing England again. After five years of depravation, humiliation, and scrounging to keep alive, here we were back home.

CHAPTER NINETEEN

Lovely daffodils for a
smashing blonde

W E landed at Greenoch in Scotland (God knows why) and were put in the Village Hall for the night...again being looked after by the Scottish Red Cross who fed us, gave us hot drinks etc. The next morning we were put onto trains and sent to Ossett near Bradford. This suited Jim, as he lived in Bradford. We were given passes to go home plus a few pounds pocket money. I eventually found myself home, to not a very good reception, as my mother had the weird idea that to be a Prisoner of War was a disgrace. She had not even told her next door neighbour that she even had a son...As I mentioned at the beginning of my story, relations between my mother and me were never a strong point, and now that I was home, I was most certainly 'in the way', as regards to her social life. She had a boyfriend. This said it all, and I spent as much time away from the house as possible. I would meet one or two of the lads that I had known before the war, and spend my time with them, only sleeping at the house, when necessary.

I went and stayed with Jim for a couple of weeks and he introduced me to a Bradford girl called Hilda. We had a good time, but she took me for every penny that I had, and when the money ran out, so did Hilda!

We were moved to a repatriation camp at Blandford in Dorset...a super camp, with every luxury. It was ten miles from Bournemouth and we were to stay here for a couple of months.

There was a good piano in the NAAFI, which I made use of I found that there were quite a few musicians in the camp, including a sergeant called Mush, who was an excellent alto sax player. We formed a band and had some great concerts etc. We wanted to hold a dance, but there was a distinct lack of girls, other than the NAAFI girls. Our Officers soon solved this little problem, by inviting the A.T.S. girls who readily accepted and came up by coach at regular intervals. It was at one of the dances that I spotted this smashing blonde. Christ, she was gorgeous! During the interval, I could not resist going over and chatting her up...she seemed to like my playing. I found out where she was billeted and it was at a rather posh hotel in Bournemouth, about 15 miles away, called The Suncliffe Hotel. I asked her if I could come to Bournemouth to see her and she agreed.

On my next day's leave, I caught a bus from Blandford to Bournemouth and arrived two hours early for my date. I had a couple of pounds in my pocket and as I was standing outside a florists shop, I saw some lovely daffodils in the window. I went in and asked if they could deliver two bunches to The Suncliffe Hotel straight away. Yes it could be done. It cost me ten shillings with delivery (50p).

An hour and a half later, I looked down the promenade and there she was, the sort of girl that you dream about, lovely blonde hair, gorgeous to look at...God, I was crazy about her. We went to a local cinema, had a fish and chip tea, and a night at the flicks. She was very pleased with the flowers that I had sent, but had been ragged rotten by the other girls. She was a lovely girl. We spent many, very happy hours together.

Soon came the great day of our de-mob (de-mobilisation). We were given civilian clothes, a ghastly light grey suit, shirts, tie, a trilby hat...we all looked like a tribe of gangsters with these dreadful clothes on.

So it was 'Home James' so to speak.

I was called to the War Crimes Commission in London to give evidence against the Germans who had hit and ill treated the Polish Children and I received a very nice letter from the Polish Ambassador thanking me for my efforts, also a nice letter from the War Office. I was told that there would possibly be some sort of commendation for my work with the Polish children from the Poles, once they had sorted themselves out after the war.

So my story comes to an end...Civvy Street...no more scrounging...no more looking behind...no more fears.

You may ask, what happened to the smashing blonde that I met?

That answer is very simple...I married her and we spent 44 very happy years together. Sadly after a long illness my lovely Brenda died on 8th February 1991. It was the saddest day of my life...I was still as much in love with her as I was when she walked down the promenade with me on our first date.

So, Dosvidanya, Kamradski, Dobranos...We are British Englanders Anglichanis.

EPILOGUE

On 28th July 1991, I was awarded the Polish Golden Cross of Merit with Swords from the Polish Government, and the coverted P.O.W. Medal, awarded for aggression to the enemy whilst a prisoner.

Lt. General H. Jubb congratulates me – also present are three Polish ladies and a representative from the Polish Government. The ladies received awards for work they did during World War Two in the Polish Underground.

In 1992, I was awarded the Chevalier's Cross in the Order of Knight of the Polish Republic.

In 1992, I was also awarded the Polish Humanitarian Medal by the Polish Government for my work with the Polish children in Zempleberg.

Easter 1993, I had a re-union with Padre Wild, (last time I saw him was in 1945). He is now 83, going strong and he said to me 'do you remember chastising the German guard who accompanied us on one of my missions, because he was scruffy and had not cleaned his boots?' How well I remembered – The Padre has published a very good book titled 'Prisoner of Hope'. It features me quite a lot and my escapades. Padre David Wild was awarded the M.B.E. and M.C. for his un-tiring work in Poland with us P.O.W.s.

Padre David Wild, M.B.E. M.C.

Letters, Awards and Citations

POLISH EMBASSY,
LONDON.

16₮ - 38

26th October, 1946.

ML/CD

Dear Sir,

In connection with the investigation of
German war crimes condu?ted by the Judge Advocate
General, certain information has been conveyed to
us concerning the ill-treatment of Polish children
near Zempelburg.

Amongst the evidence which was supplied to us
we have found your name and learned of your attitude
in connection with the sad events which took place
in Zempelburg.

I am writing to you in order to convey to you
my appreciation and thanks for the attitude which
you displayed in the defence of poor and helpless
children, against whom the Germans launched a most
brutal attack.   This humane action of yours
undoubtedly gave to those children a ray of hope
and some evidence that human feeling had not
altogether disappeared.

Yours faithfully,

/J. Winiewicz/.
Chargé d'Affaires a.i.

PREZYDENT RZECZYPOSPOLITEJ POLSKIEJ (na Uchodzstwie)

PRESIDENT OF THE REPUBLIC OF POLAND (in Exile)

POLISH HONOURS AWARDED VIA THE REPUBLIC OF POLAND (IN EXILE)

UNDER THE OLD CONSTITUTION OF 23rd. APRIL 1935, WHICH CEASED 20th. DECEMBER 1990, WHEN THE NEW POLISH REPUBLIC OF POLAND CAME INTO BEING UNDER LECH WALESA.

1. Gold Cross of Merit with Swords to Mr Eric Williams, 107 James Reckitt Avenue, Hull.HU8 7JT. Ex.4th.Batt. East Yorkshire Regt. 50 TT Div. III Army B.E.F. Captured at Boulogne,France,May 1940. P.O.W. Poland June 1940 - May 1945. Resisting the enemy whilst P.O.W. and helping Polish children.

Rzeczpospolita Polska

PREZES RADY MINISTRÓW

For..
Lieut. Gen. Chev. H. Jubb PAF.

LIEUT. GENERAL H. JURD, P.A.F.
CHIEF ADVISOR ON COMBATTANTS AFFAIRS
TO H.E. THE PRESIDENT OF THE
REPUBLIC OF POLAND (IN EXILE)

88

CHANCELLOR OF THE ORDER OF POLONIA RESTITUTA

certifies
that
THE PRESIDENT OF THE REPUBLIC
(in Exile)
by Decree of

20.12.1990

for

support given to the Polish
Government in Exile
included

Eric Williams

in the roll of the

KNIGHTS OF THE ORDER OF
POLONIA RESTITUTA

by awarding him

Chevalier's Cross

of this Order

PREZYDENT RZECZYPOSPOLITEJ
PRESIDENT OF THE REPUBLIC

KANCLERZ
CHANCELLOR

DANIEL ZDRUJEWSKI

DYPLOM

Prezydent
Rzeczypospolitej Polskiej
na wniosek Rady Ministrów — nadal

ERIC WILLIAMS

KRZYZ ZA **WOLNOŚĆ I NIEPODLEGŁOŚĆ**
Z MIECZAMI

za participation in the fight for Independence of Poland during 2nd world war 1939-
1945

W OKRESIE DRUGIEJ WOJNY ŚWIATOWEJ 1939 - 1945

PREZES RADY MINISTROW

LONDYN, dnia Twentieth December 19 90 r.